PIERRE DEUX'S

Paris Country

PIERRE DEUX'S
Paris Country
A STYLE AND SOURCE BOOK OF THE ILE-DE-FRANCE

BY LINDA DANNENBERG,
PIERRE LEVEC,
AND PIERRE MOULIN

Photographs by Guy Bouchet
Design by Paul Hardy

CLARKSON POTTER, PUBLISHERS/NEW YORK

To Steve and Benjamin: The high point of every trip is coming home to them.

—*Linda Dannenberg*

We are proud to dedicate this book to these loyal employees who helped put it all together, led by our talented girl Friday in Paris, Isabelle Pilate, who prepared the ground for us so very well. Over the years, all the associates named below have done more than their share to help us:

Susan Allyson, John Baer, John Bermingham, Ann Bos, Serge Bisono, Diane Carroll, Terence Cochran, Jon and Mira De Deus, Pierrette Deport, Robert Diffenderfer, Berte Fink, Randy Fisher, David Frost, Barbara Golden, David Graham, Alice Hawes, Stephen Jiavis, Elliott Johnson, Judanne Jones, Mary Konakowitz, Anka and Henri Lefebvre (also Carol, Henri Junior and Patrick Lefebvre), Gail Levine, Anne Liberator, Maxine McCorkle, Chris Meason, Matthew Meyers, Becky Newcomer, Wendy Newcomer, Bette Nigro, Jeanne Pierre, Connie and Gus Penteck, Diana Peebles, Willard Pitt, Sonia Rivelli, Christine Roberts, Pam Ryder, Gerhild Schendl, Laura Soelter, Joan Stevenson, Shirley Thompson, Kathy Turman, Barbara Zauft.

We offer a special bow to Lupe De La Garza, who has passed on.

Our sincere thanks to all. Without you our salutes to the provinces of France would never have waved so proudly.

—*Pierre LeVec*
and Pierre Moulin

Text Copyright © 1991 by Linda Dannenberg, Pierre LeVec, and Pierre Moulin
Photographs copyright © 1991 by Guy Bouchet

Published by Clarkson N. Potter, Inc., 201 East 50th Street, New York, New York 10022, and distributed by Crown Publishers, Inc.
Member of the Crown Publishers Group.

CLARKSON N. POTTER, POTTER and colophon are trademarks of Clarkson N. Potter, Inc.

Manufactured in Japan

Library of Congress Cataloging-in-Publication Data
Dannenberg, Linda.
  Pierre Deux's Paris Country: a style and source book of the Ile-de-France/by Linda Dannenberg, Pierre LeVec, and Pierre Moulin.—1st ed.
     p. cm
  1. Decoration and ornament, Rustic—France—Ile-de-France. 2. Interior decoration—France—Ile-de-France.
3. Ile-de-France—Social life and customs.
I. LeVec, Pierre. II. Moulin, Pierre.
III. Pierre Deux (Firm) IV. Title.
NK1449.A314734   1991
745.4′494434—dc20   90-38539
                                  CIP

ISBN 0-517-56436-X

10 9 8 7 6 5 4 3 2 1

First Edition

ACKNOWLEDGMENTS

The Ile-de-France, which we visited frequently during the two years we researched, photographed, and wrote this book, charmed us with its grace, harmony, and refined style. Each sortie out from Paris—and there were scores of them—brought intriguing discoveries. There were wonderful restaurants, superb homes, handsome château-museums, and always the gentle, lovely countryside of this province that encircles Paris in a snug embrace. The deepest and most lasting pleasures we experienced during this project, and which we carry with us still, were the friendships and acquaintanceships we made photographing the many homes and sights presented in the following pages. We found the warmth and generosity of the people who opened their homes and lives to us, and shared their contacts and ideas with us, very moving. The most important components of a lifestyle book are the people portrayed within, living life with style. To these people, and to the many others who participated in the creation of this book, we would like to express our appreciation and gratitude.

For their hospitality, their friendship, and their cooperation in Paris and the Ile-de-France, we are most grateful to: Philippe Lachaux and Claude Aucouturier; Sebastien Hemmeler; Birgitta and Olivier Fouret; Philippe Gribinski and Abigail de Vivie; Geneviève Prou; Jean-Pierre and Henri Scoffier of Les Préjugés; Charles D'Ussel; Yolande Castel; Marc and Germaine Camoletti; Jean-Louis Lécart; Jean-François Gosselin; Yves Bienaimé of Chantilly's

Musée Vivant du Cheval; Charles de Yturbe of Château D'Anet; Josette Brédif of the Musée Oberkampf in Jouy-en-Josas; Fabrizio Ruspoli and Philippe Cluzel; Monsieur and Madame Claudel; Claudette Lindsey of Giverny's Musée Claude Monet; Pierre and Isabelle Chalvignac; Mireille Lothon; General and Comtesse J. L. du Temple de Rougemont; Flavie Chaillet of Hermès; Monsieur Courteaux-Enault; Monsieur and Madame Le Normand; Monsieur Ariès and Madame Ariès of the Musée de Sceaux; Marquise de Lastic; Anne de Lacretelle; Monsieur Chaux, director of L'Ecole d'Horticulture et Paysage; Monsieur de Lalonde; Françoise Ledoux-Wernert; Madame de St. Sienne; Magy Bocquet; Ramuntcho de Saint-Amand; Madame Crapet; Celine Nguyen; Olivia Phelip; Lillian Williams; and Pierre de Regaini.

To our friends and colleagues in New York, for their generous help, participation, and support: Gayle Benderoff and Deborah Geltman, our fine agents, for proposing, interceding, and expediting so expertly on our behalf; our enthusiastic and informative liaisons at the French Cultural Tourist Office, Michel Bouquier, George Hern, and Marion Fourestier; Spencer Hardy, for Stateside photographs so professionally produced; our inspired mapmaker, Oliver Williams; and Nancy Novogrod, for her early input and continued interest in our Living In France series.

To members of the Pierre Deux family for their help in an infinite variety of ways: Serge Bisono, David Frost, Anka Lefebvre, Barbara Zauft, David Graham, and Robert Diffendorfer.

To Isabelle Pilate, a special thank-you, for her devotion, as much as for her thorough and tireless help in researching and documenting information integral to this book.

To Sylvia Etendart, a remarkable, longtime friend and distinguished *antiquaire,* our heartfelt gratitude for her generosity, her hospitality, and for the benefit of her knowledge and expertise in the domain of fine French furniture.

To Paul Hardy, our designer on this book as well as on *French Country, Pierre Deux's Normandy,* and *Pierre Deux's Brittany,* who creates out of the chaos of thousands of pictures and tens of thousands of words a cohesive whole that captures, between two covers, the spirit and ambiance of a special place.

To Guy Bouchet, wonderful friend and superb photographer, who brings to his work an irrepressible spirit, a distinctive warmth, and an exquisite sense of composition.

To Lauren Shakely, our clear-eyed and ever-patient editor, who expertly guided us through the shoals and squalls of creativity, helping us, as she did on *Pierre Deux's Normandy* and *Pierre Deux's Brittany,* to achieve our vision.

And to other friends and colleagues at Clarkson N. Potter and Crown Publishers, for their support, guidance, and inspiration, as always: Carol Southern, Bruce Harris, Howard Klein, Michelle Sidrane, Barbara Marks, Tina Zabriskie, Phyllis Fleiss, Jonathan Fox, Teresa Nicholas, Lisa Lawley, and Allan Eady.

Merci infiniment à tous!

CONTENTS

Impressions of the Ile-de-France

Life comme il faut—*graciousness and good taste are by-words in the Ile-de-France.* Left, *thick ivy blankets the facade of a graceful estate only 10 miles west of Paris. A mother shepherds her children,* above, *to an alfresco birthday party in Versaille's Balbi Park.*

THE ILE-DE-FRANCE IS A STATE OF MIND AS MUCH AS IT IS A PLACE, A PASTORAL DREAM OF THE PARISIAN COUNTRYSIDE.

This ancient heart-land of France, literally the "Island of France," surrounds Paris, its outer limits just one or two hours' driving time from the capital. Originally much smaller, the region was so named because it was circumscribed by five rivers—the Marne, the Aisne, the Seine, the Oise, and the Ourcq—that created a large, landlocked "island" north of Paris. Among the well-known names that distinguish the area's map are Chantilly, Versailles, Barbizon, and Fontainebleau. Here are handsome architecture, graceful landscapes, renowned forests, an abundance of rivers and streams, and neatly groomed towns. There is an *esprit Ile-de-France* that exists nowhere else—a grace, harmony, and charm that are subtly modulated by a concern for appearances and a desire to conform. Very little is startling, ostentatious, or out of place in the Ile-de-France.

One of the most striking aspects of the Ile-de-France is that in spite of encroaching high-rises, malls, and planned communities radiating outward from the urban hub, it is still predominantly pastoral. Just beyond the city limits, suburban sprawl is redefining the regional character, but 30 to 40 minutes' driving time from the heart of Paris the industrial com-

plexes and housing developments suddenly give way to broad open fields and forests, with silhouettes of small stone villages and imposing châteaux in the distance. Driving on the back-

The mairie (town hall), *left, dominates a small town en route to Provins, southeast of Paris. Bright fields of* colza (rape) *color the landscape throughout the provinces,* right.

Gisors

Creil

Senlis

Crépy-en-Valois

Magny-en-Vexin

Chantilly

ABBAYE DE ROYAUMONT

Pontoise

Conflans-Ste-Honorine

Mantes-la-Jolie

Poissy

Maisons-Laffitte

Enghien-les-Bains

Meaux

Jouarre

St-Germain-en-Laye

St-Cloud

St-Denis

PARIS

Houdan

Thoiry

Sèvres

Nogent-sur-Marne

Coulommiers

Bois d'Arcy

Sceaux

Montfort-l'Amaury

VERSAILLES

Jouy-en-Josas

Choisy-le-Roi

Brie-Comte-Robert

La Ferté-Gaucher

Dampierre

Chevreuse

Rosay-en-Brie

Rambouillet

Montlhéry

Corbeil-Essonnes

Vaux-le-Vicomte

Provins

Dourdan

La Ferté-Alais

Melun Sénart

Bois-le-Roi

Rampillon

Chartres

Etampes

Courances

Barbizon

Fontainebleau

Méréville

Milly-la-Forêt

Moret-sur-Loing

Nemours

Pithiviers

Château-Landon

Sens

roads of this province in the shadow of Notre Dame, one discovers remarkable villages such as Provins, along the D *(départementale)* 106, or Fleury-en-Bière on the D11, virtually untouched by time. The transition is remarkable.

The signature landscape of the Ile-de-France is flat—vast stretches of farmland relieved by gentle hills and modest valleys to the west and east. Broad fields of wheat, preserves of woodland, and tracts of brilliant yellow *colza,* or rape, blend into a patchwork of beige, green, and yellow. Protected forests shade enormous stretches of the Ile-de-France—the Forest of Rambouillet, the Forest of Fontainebleau, the Forest of Saint-Germain among them—giving this province a light-dappled quality of ro-

mance. The tangle of sinuous rivers that gave the province its name, along with countless tributaries, flow toward or away from the great Mother River, the Seine, their banks bordered by willow. *Péniches,* the river barges that are increasingly popular for meandering tours of the region, inch their way upstream through the placid landscape.

Agriculturally rich, the Ile-de-France is also plentiful in wild game, especially deer, rabbit, and boar. In the fall, the forests echo with the sounds of hunting horns during the seasonal *chasse à courre,* with aristocratic hunters mounted on horseback, accom-

panied by their packs of yapping hounds, pursuing the fauna of the Ile-de-France.

The kingdom of France began here in the outskirts of Paris. More than any other province in France, the Ile-de-France boasts a distinctly royal heritage. While the history of the Ile-de-France extends back hundreds of years before Christ, when it was settled by tribes of Celts, and continues in the time of Julius Caesar, when Paris was a Gallo-Roman city called Lutèce, its "modern" history begins in A.D. 486 when the Merovingian warrier Clovis defeated the Roman armies and became king of the new land he

The heart of France, the Ile-de-France is almost an island surrounded by rivers, left. *Paris is never far away from any point in the Ile-de-France,* above. *In Chantilly, the hunt is still an annual event,* right. Overleaf: *pastoral impressions of the Ile-de-France.*

called Francia, the original France. After Clovis there followed a succession of kings and dynasties that included Charlemagne's reign as Holy King of France from 768 to 814. But it is Hugues Capet, duke and suzerain of a vast territory that made up the original Ile-de-France, who is regarded as the true founder of the French royal house. Chosen king of France by a gathering of feudal barons in 987 at Senlis, Capet fathered a line of descendants who ruled France, with the exception of a 21-year period after the Revolution, until 1848—almost 900 years.

The history of the Ile-de-France, the heart of the French nation, is the history of France itself. Royal influence and a rich royal legacy distinguish the look of the prov-

ince today. The magnificent gardens designed by landscape architect André Le Nôtre in Versailles, Fontainebleau, and Chantilly, the great reservoirs and aqueducts commissioned by Louis XIV in Marly and Maintenon, the traditional hunting grounds on ancient seigneurial domains, and finally the virtual embarrassment of châteaux in the styles of Louis XIV, XV, and XVI are all striking reminders of the Ile-de-France's noble *temps*

perdu. The past embellishes the present here in a way unmatched by any other of France's historically rich provinces.

In some ways the Ile-de-France is a paradox. It is provincial and yet, because of its proximity to Paris, sophisticated. It has a rich aristocratic history and an equally important agricultural tradition. In architecture the Ile-de-France presents several regional styles: half-timbered houses or stone cottages like those of Normandy and Brittany, brick houses similar to those in Picardy, limestone châteaux that rival those in the Loire Valley, and farmhouses similar to those seen in Burgundy. Yet there is still an atmosphere, an "everything-in-its-place" look, a mood that prompts admirers to describe a house, a garden, or a town as *"très Ile-de-France."* Neat, lovely, but not overwhelming gardens of traditional fragrant flowers such as lilacs, lilies of the valley, or roses; houses in scale and tone with their landscape—these are the region's tasteful trademarks.

Bastille Day is an important holiday in the region, above. In clipped topiary hedges and carefully maintained walks, the Ile-de-France shows its refinement, left. A gardener keeps the complex patterns of boxwood in perfect trim in the gardens of the Château de Champs, right.

In a characteristic image of the Ile-de-France, left, a vast landscape of wheat stretches to the horizon in the northwestern part of the province. A baby lamb pauses in play, above, at the Bergerie Nationale in Rambouillet.

A couple strolls up an allée *of linden trees on a Sunday in the town of Marly-le-Roi,* left. *Preceding pages: An aristocratic past still characterizes the Ile-de-France of today, with sumptuous wrought-iron portals, elegant topiary gardens, graceful* allées, *and timeless noble architecture.*

PART ONE

Le Grand Style

ELEGANCE AND RESTRAINT

A graceful wrought-iron grille, characteristic of sumptuous dwellings in the Ile-de-France, encloses the Château de Villiers-le-Mahieu, a 17th-century estate recently converted into a small hotel, left. Members of France's elite Garde Républicaine, above, sound the fanfare that signals the beginning of festivities at the Prix de Diane.

AS THE HEART OF THE KINGDOM FROM MEDIEVAL TIMES, THE ILE-DE-FRANCE IS THE MOST SOPHISTICATED OF THE FRENCH PROVINCES, WHERE WEALTH IS ALWAYS TEMPERED BY NOBLE RESTRAINT.

In the environs of Paris, the king and his court retreated to châteaux and hunting lodges, erected the great cathedrals of Saint-Denis and Chartres and endowed vast monasteries. The best-known display of *"le grand style"* is the palace of Versailles, begun by Louis XIII in 1631 and surrendered when the French Revolution brought down the monarchy in 1789. But elements of the style may be found all over the province, whether in the elegant curves of a bombé bureau or the crisp lines of a boxwood garden. In the Ile-de-France it is easy to imagine the grandeur of the realm, the refined heights of style that admirers all over the world consider to be "French."

The most elegant and fashionable suburban towns of the Ile-de-France have best survived the encroaching modernization radiating outward from Paris. Most of these are located to the west of Paris in the Yvelines or Hauts-de-Seine *départements*—Maisons-Laffitte, Saint-Germain-en-Laye, Bougival, Marnes-la-Coquette, Sèvres, Meudon, Marly-le-Roi, and, of course, Versailles, with its innumerable riches. All manage to retain their distinctive character in an area losing its charm to the inevitable advance of the city.

A table is set for luncheon, left, *at the Prix de Diane in Chantilly. Diane de Poitiers appears,* above left, *in a portrait that hangs in the Château d'Anet. Sculpted cherubs, such as these on the grounds of a 17th-century château near Rambouillet,* above, *and classical Greek seminudes, such as the wheat-bearing female figure,* right, *at the Château de Villiers-le-Mahieu, are popular adornments in the parks of grand estates.*

DOUCEUR DE VIVRE

The Château de la Motte-Tilly, on the outskirts of Provins in the southeastern corner of the Ile-de-France, commands a vast 160-acre property of groomed parks, ponds, and woodland. The château was the home of Aliette de Rohan-Chabot, the marquise de Maillé, who left it as her legacy to France at her death in 1972. Since then it has been preserved, just as she left it, as a château-museum and a *monument historique* by the French government. (The French government preserves and protects hundreds of landmark châteaux, public buildings, and other architectural masterworks— the abbey of Mont Saint-Michel, the Château Vaux-le-Vicomte, and the Place des Vosges in Paris among them—either by purchasing them or receiving them as outright bequests and maintaining them as museums, or by providing restoration funds for the upkeep and repair of still private dwellings. Most of these latter properties must, in return for the financial aid, be open to the public, either by appointment or during set visiting hours.) The estate's unusual name, used since the 14th century, is a compilation of old French and Celtic: la Motte from the French word for a fortified feudal structure, and Tilly

A paradigm of sober elegance, the 18th-century Château de la Motte-Tilly evokes the grandeur and graciousness of its epoch with its handsome slate roof, brick-and-sandstone facade, and wrought-iron window grilles— all conceived by the architect François-Nicholas Lancret.

from Tillede or Tilli, the Celtic word for the *tilleuls* (linden trees) that line the banks of the nearby Seine.

High wrought-iron gates flanked by small, elegant gatehouse pavilions open onto this imposing estate. The château's front, or southern facade—its public face—overlooks a wide graveled courtyard; the rear surveys a long sloping vista, with gently terraced esplanades and gardens *à la française* descending to a large reflecting pool fed by the Seine.

For the marquise de Maillé, her château evoked the *"douceur de vivre"* (the gracious lifestyle) of the 18th century that she sought to recapture in her assiduous, pure 18th-century redecoration of the estate. Like many châteaux of the epoch (it was built in 1755), the Château de la Motte-Tilly is the embodiment of sober elegance, with its harmonious proportions worked in the finest brick, slate, and sandstone by artisans who were true masters of their trade. Commissioned by two noble brothers, Pierre Terray de Rozières and l'Abbé Joseph-Marie Terray, who razed a medieval château that still existed on the property, the château was designed by the architect François-Nicolas Lancret. Shortly after the Revolution, less than four decades from its conception, La Motte-Tilly was sacked and pillaged. In 1910, after years of neglect, it was bought

A graceful Louis XV banquette with a leather seat, created in the Ile-de-France, left, *sits in quiet harmony with the neutral tones of a second-floor hall landing. In a corner of the* bibliothèque, right, *three Louis XV chairs with upholstered seats surround a Louis XV game table. In the foreground is a generously proportioned tapestry-covered chair of the same period.*

and totally restored to its 18th-century glory by the comte Gérard de Rohân-Chabot, a descendant of the Terray family.

The daughter and lone heir to the fortune of the comte de Rohan-Chabot, the marquise de Maillé, totally refurbished the château after the death of her father in 1964. Although she installed central heating, in every other aspect she created a harmonious period piece. She searched out the best furniture of the ancien régime, adding to the already considerable collection of family heirlooms in the château and eliminating virtually all furniture created after 1800. The exacting marquise wanted each piece to represent the best of French taste. She worked unstintingly at her project until she died from an accidental fall in November 1972.

The château today is just as the late Aliette de Rohan-Chabot left it: her family photographs adorn her desk and the mantel of her study; the dining room table is set with her favorite plates. Her presence and her remarkable taste are pervasive, which was her great wish and her generous legacy.

Furnished and decorated by the comte de Rohan-Chabot, the father of the marquise de Maillé, the bibliothèque *is a comfortable mix of museum-quality 18th-century antiques and some modern pieces. It was here that the last resident, the marquise de Maillé, liked to receive her guests. The oval-framed portrait on the far wall is of Jeanne Terray de Morel-Vindé, the marquise's grandmother.*

Subtly painted Louis XVI boiserie panels the walls of the dining room, left, whose tall windows overlook the courtyard. The painted panels above the doorways, depicting mythological gods, were created in 1922 by the French artist Maillard after the originals in the Hôtel de Soubise, a 17th-century landmark mansion in Paris. Surrounding the table are a set of carved and painted Regency chairs. The 18th-century Orléans porcelain table service, above, carries the monogram of the Rohan-Soubise family. The table is set in 18th-century fashion—implements face down, with handles toward the center of the table.

One of the most elegant rooms in the château, the Salon Bleu is the only room in the residence with boiserie that was part of the château's original 18th-century décor. The sculpted moldings are subtly highlighted by two shades of blue. Among the room's superb 18th-century furniture is a small oval table in the center of the photograph, signed J. P. Dusantoy, a master furniture maker in the time of Louis XV.

The sumptuously upholstered velvet sofa is detailed in the elegant swags and tassels favored during the epoch of Louis XVI. To the right of the sofa, a painted 18th-century screen with a chinoiserie motif repeats the room's color scheme of blue and gold.

Depicting aristocrats lunching at a riverside tavern, the 18th-century painted panel, left, set into the boiserie is one of several charming naive representations of country life in the Ile-de-France displayed throughout the house. The portrait below shows an 18th-century princesse de Beauvau, a member of the Rohan-Chabot family. Set before a naive painted screen in the Grand Salon, right, is one of four Louis XV grands fauteuils of very high quality upholstered in green velour.

Dominating the Salle de Billiard (Billiard Room), right, is a rare and monumental billiard table in dazzling marquetry, dated 1839. Among the table's intricately inset designs are the 12 signs of the zodiac, seen here in detail, above. Even the cues are inset with elegantly detailed floral and figurative motifs.

One of the château's original bathrooms was transformed into a salon de coiffure, *literally a room where ladies were coiffed by their maids and completed their* toilettes. *Set before the Louis XV* coiffeuse, or dressing table, *is a low Louis XVI chair. Against the wall in the background is an 18th-century leather* chaise-bidet. *Surveying the room from his faux* marbre niche *is a Louis XIV statue of* Amour.

Each of the château's bedrooms is decorated in a distinctly individual style. The bedroom created for the marquise's daughter, Claire-Clémence, is a bright, airy, feminine room with predominantly Louis XV furniture and a canopied bed, left. In the Chambre Empire, below left, the furniture and fabrics are all from Napoleon's Imperial years of 1804 to 1815. The room is the exception to the rule of 18th-century furnishings that prevails in the château. The Empire furniture is all in mahogany—very fashionable at the time —and the toile de Jouy is a reproduction of a fabric created during this epoch. The sculpted Greek marble head on the desk, dating from the Hellenistic period, was discovered in Rome in 1922 behind the Coliseum.

Just off the bedroom of the marquise is her generously proportioned bathroom. The bathing area, which can be enclosed by the blue-and-white toile curtains, is painted in faux marbre. The two large mirrors create an illusion of greater space.

In the marquise's bedroom, her Louis XVI bed is set into a sumptuous sleeping alcove with boiserie subtly painted in shades of cream and pale gray. Beyond the door to the right with the mullioned glass panes is the bathroom. The door to the left opens into a closet.

45

TOILE DE JOUY

If one fabric had to be chosen to represent the Republic of France, it would have to be toile de Jouy, the classic, oft-imitated linen-textured cottons with elaborate monochromatic prints in red, blue, green, black, or brown on an off-white background. First produced in the mid–18th century by Christophe-Philippe Oberkampf in the town of Jouy-en-Josas, near Versailles, the fabrics, with their elegant patterns of historic or allegorical scenes or pastoral landscapes, were an instant success with the court and local aristocracy. Louis XV and then Louis XVI supported the production house, which officially became a *manufacture royale* in 1783. In the early years the lengths of newly printed fabric were laid out to dry in the surrounding fields, creating a huge patchwork of toile de Jouy that must have captivated passing noblemen on their way to court.

The haut monde of the ancien régime kept the *manufacture* running at full production. A continuous stream of noble coaches carried away from Jouy a fortune in fabrics every day. The toiles were used to cover walls, upholster chairs, curtain windows,

Historic correspondence and pages from a 19th-century order book in the collection of the Musée Oberkampf form a still life with an original 18th-century toile de Jouy print. The letter, dated four years after the Revolution, begins "Citoyen" (Citizen).

and adorn bedsteads with sumptuous "tents," canopies, and headboards. Many châteaux and manor houses of the period—today museums, hotels, or still private residences—bear witness to the popularity of toile de Jouy for more than half a century. Strong, heavy, and colorfast, the 18th- and 19th-century toiles, exposed to air, light, and dust for decades, some for almost 200 years, are still handsome. One of the best places to view the handsome old toiles is the small Musée Oberkampf, a museum dedicated to toile fabrics, lodged in a château in Jouy-en-Josas.

Originally printing with hand-carved wood blocks when he installed his operation in Jouy in 1760, Oberkampf switched to engraved copper plates, and then cylinders, as soon as the technique was developed. Industrially advanced, the company produced 11 million yards of toile by the end of the 18th century, becoming the largest and most important fabric house in Europe. Oberkampf's success spawned competitors throughout Europe but none of them could equal the work of the master, largely because of his company's superiority in designs. Oberkampf's top fabric designer was Jean-Baptiste Huet, many of whose classic designs, with titles such as "Lafayette—Hommage de l'Amérique à la France," and "Visite du Port de

Juxtaposed with 18th-century planches *(carved blocks for hand-printing fabric) and some tools of the trade, an Empire-era fabric is rich in the classical motifs popular during Napoleon's glory days. Napoleon, fond of the Jouy fabrics, awarded their creator, Christophe-Philippe Oberkampf, the Légion d'Honneur in 1806.*

Cherbourg par Louis XVI," are still being produced today. His pastoral themes and "storytelling" toiles in particular caught the fancy of the trendy court community; in the same spirit as Marie-Antoinette's Hameau, the bucolic toile images must have offered a pleasant counterpoint to the surfeit of formal elegance at Versailles.

The heyday of toile de Jouy lasted until the collapse of Napoleon's Empire in 1815, and with it the decline of the French economy. Oberkampf died the same year, at the age of 77. For the remainder of the 19th century and early 20th, there was little demand for the fabrics; tastes had changed. The factories closed and the machines fell into disrepair, or were melted down, and the only toiles de Jouy available were inferior reproductions. But today the fabrics live again. After a long search in the provinces, Pierre Deux found an 18th-century printing machine, a collection of 18th-century etched copper cylinders, and an Alsatian printer able to use the machines. Classic toiles de Jouy are now produced exactly as they were 200 years ago. The renaissance of toile de Jouy would have made Oberkampf proud.

A handsome, haunting toile de Jouy of the Empire period, created in 1808, commemorates Napoleon's Egyptian expedition of 1798 to 1799. The fabric, contrast-bordered with an India print fabric, was once part of a curtain in a château's salon.

A *fauteuil in the Musée Ober-kampf in Jouy-en-Josas,* left, *is slipcovered in a red-and-white toile created in the 1820s. A variety of print styles and themes— pastoral, rustic, romantic, historic, and floral—was created in Jouy-en-Josas between the years 1760 and 1843,* right.

ABBAYE DE ROYAUMONT

The Abbaye de Royaumont—a vast property made up of a refectory, a cloister, a chapel, a great hall, a farm, and the remains of a 13th-century church—is one of the grandest monasteries in the Ile-de-France, an area rich in religious enclaves thanks to the generosity of royal benefactors. Partially demolished after the Revolution (the church was razed and a cotton mill set up in the remaining buildings), the abbey was acquired by the Soeurs de la Société Famille de Bordeaux (Sisters of the Bordeaux Family Society), who began the restoration, and later by the Gouin family, the present owners, who bought the property at the turn of this century and continued the extensive restoration. Although not entirely its former self—only one wall, a stair tower, and partial pillars remain of the 13th-century church —the abbey as it stands today nevertheless reflects the power it once enjoyed.

The abbey was conceived by Louis VIII, known as Louis the Lion, who never lived to see its construction. In his will he charged his son, Louis IX, the revered Saint Louis, to inaugurate the construction of a monastery at the Royaumont site. Only 12 years old at the time he commissioned the abbey in 1228, Saint Louis consecrated the completed enclave to the memory of his father seven years later. Powerful yet austere, Royaumont was built for an order of Cistercian monks, a branch of the Benedictine order that shunned the ornate and the lavish in religious construction. A cultural center now, the abbey is the site of concerts, lectures, and art exhibits. Music and erudite chatter emanate from the superb cloister, the ancient refectory, and the library that once harbored generations of Cistercian brothers, predecessors of the Trappists.

A sense of timeless serenity pervades the property of the Abbaye de Royaumont, inset, *the 13th-century monastery founded by Saint Louis, the beloved king Louis IX. A cultural center today, the abbey enclave maintains a distinctly ecclesiastical air throughout its gardens and buildings. Conically clipped cedars stand sentry around the ancient cloister,* above, *while a system of small streams, feeders to the river Thève, reflects the facade's imposing Gothic windows,* right.

THE CHATEAU D'ANET

Château d'Anet, a 30-minute drive west of Versailles, is a testimony to the high level of architectural design in the 16th century. It took five years of intensive labor to construct this treasure, commissioned by Diane de Poitiers, the duchess of Valentinois, but better known as the mistress of Henri II, in 1547. The architect, Philibert Delorme, supervised the design, assisted by a handful of other architects and artists, among them the Renaissance goldsmith Benvenuto Cellini.

Diane de Poitiers was the beautiful young widow of Count Louis

Château d'Anet's chapel, above, *was completed in 1552. Precise geometric gardens,* left, *enhance paths through the courtyard. The triumphal arched portal that leads into the 16th-century château,* right, *designed by Philibert Delorme, was conceived as an homage to Diana, goddess of the hunt, but in fact was designed to please the chatelaine, Diane de Poitiers.*

de Brézé, a powerful noble 40 years her senior. At her husband's side, while still a teenager, she learned to ride and hunt, skills that brought her renown for the rest of her life. She was often portrayed in paintings and sculptures as a huntress, and motifs of the hunt—stags, hunting dogs, arrows, and crescent moons, symbols of the mythological Diana—appear throughout the château. Also ubiquitous are Diane's initials and those of Henri II, occasionally interlocked. Henri fell in love with Diane when he was barely 15 years old and she was in her early thirties. What began as

The chapel of the Château d'Anet, left, was one of architect Delorme's favorite creations. The floor, which repeats the rosette design of the ceiling, is inlaid with precious marble that once graced the floors of villas belonging to Roman emperors. The bas-reliefs of angels carrying symbols of the Passion are by 16th-century sculptor Jean Goujon. The statues of the Apostles niched beneath them are attributed to Germain Pilon. Since 1944, Charles de Yturbe, below, and his wife have been tirelessly restoring their landmark property.

an adolescent crush evolved into a profound love that lasted through his marriage to Catherine de Medicis and his coronation, ending only at his accidental death in a tourney in 1559.

Construction of Château d'Anet, conceived as a luxurious country retreat and an intimate love nest, commenced in the year that Henri became king. In contrast to other ornate châteaux in the region, commissioned by men, Diane's Anet has a marked female influence, particularly in the graceful, refined, even romantic décor.

A luminous, exquisitely detailed chapel with angelic bas-reliefs encircling a domed rose window is still the setting for small religious services for neighboring townsfolk and château staff. To the right of the main portal is a lavish funerary chapel built by Diane's daughter, Louise de Brézé, as a final resting place for her mother, who died at the age of 67 in 1566. Sadly, during the Revolution, Diane's tomb was desecrated, her remains thrown into a ditch, and her sarcophagus dragged to a nearby farm for use as a pig trough.

Restoration was begun in 1840 by Count Adolphe de Caraman and continued by Ferdinand Moreau, a government deputy, and his descendants, Monsieur and Madame Charles de Yturbe, who are the current residents of this once-again splendid *monument historique.*

The chapel's magnificent central dome was one of the first ever constructed in France. More than 200 caissons (square sculpted panels) rise to the central aperture. The design was conceived to give the impression of a circular movement up to heaven.

ART OF THE EBENISTE

In this province permeated by the trends of the court of Versailles and the aristocracy, regional furniture and many decorative accessories were directly influenced by the seminal décors of the kings Louis—XIII, XIV, XV, and XVI. Designers of the Regency and Directoire, Napoleons I and III, and Louis Philippe periods also imposed their tastes. Over the centuries, France's premier *ébénistes* (cabinetmakers) created for their royal and noble clients the exquisite furniture that inspired design throughout Europe and continues to be reproduced today. These same royal craftsmen sometimes accepted commissions from humbler clients, producing furniture with similar lines, quality, and sophistication but in solid wood—often the fine-grained local oak—rather than in marquetry and gilt.

The region's proximity to Paris precluded the development of an identifiably regional style, such as there is in other provinces—a *style Normand,* a *style Breton,* a *style Provençal.* Well-made, graceful, and somewhat reserved, provincial furniture from Ile-de-France is characterized by local woods—wild cherry, beech, and other fruitwoods—sober lines,

In the Château de Champs, now a state-owned museum, two caned Louis XV chairs await players for a chesslike game introduced to the court by Louis XV.

Suggesting evenings of entertainment at court are the powdered wig on a stand and the yellow silk frock coat of an important noble laid out on an 18th-century gilded banquette or harpsichord bench in the Grand Salon of the Château de Champs.

and simple, graceful motifs and moldings. The style of Louis XV was popular in provincial furniture through most of the 18th century and was superseded by the style of Louis XVI only after the turn of the 19th century.

At the outer reaches of the province, furniture making was also influenced by the styles of the neighboring provinces—Normandy to the west, Picardy to the north, Champagne to the east, and Burgundy to the south. Everywhere, the furniture-making process was long and complex. It took at least seven years just to prepare the wood, first by immersing it in water to take out the "play" and sometimes smoking it to protect it against worms.

Traditional pieces produced in other provinces of France are also found in the Ile-de-France: *coffres* and *pétrins* (storage chests and flouring tables); armoires, both tall and of medium height; caned chairs and rectangular harvest tables; *buffets bas* (low buffet cabinets); *buffets à deux-corps* (chest-on-chests); *vaisseliers* (china cabinets or étagères); *meubles d'angle* (corner cabinets); and small commodes and drop-leaf desks. Furniture was either highly polished or painted, usually in soft gray or gray-blue with paler trim. Embellishing some of the more ornate pieces are sculpted sheaves of wheat, rosette motifs, and baskets of flowers.

A brocade-covered Louis XVI duchesse *regally commands a living-room corner in a château near Fontainebleau,* left. *Very Ile-de-France, the finely crafted* duchesse, *like much of the furniture created in the region, is quite sophisticated, and was inspired by the furniture of the court. The fabric of the walls, curtains, and folding screen is by Braquenié. The small, ornate box,* right, *is a* boîte à perruques *(wig box) crafted in the 18th century.*

A stone architectural element from the late 18th or early 19th century, *below*, greets visitors to the marble-tiled grand entry hall of the Château de Champs. The luster of bronze and crystal lights up the dining room, *right*, laid for dinner in the 18th-century manner, with cutlery on the right of the plate and fork tines turned down. The dining table is surrounded by transition-style caned-back chairs.

A duchesse *(a small, elegant daybed)* allowed a relaxed position near the fire, above, *in the Château de Champs' salon, which is lined with boiserie painted in cameo blue. A detail of one of the salon's panels,* right, *shows a rural scene.*

At the Paris Biennale des Tissus, the biannual Paris fabrics show, a model room by Manuel Canovas, above, recreates the intimacy of an 18th-century boudoir, with a lit à la Polonaise (the swagged and pillowed daybed), an elegant coiffeuse (dressing table) adorned with candelabra, and two painted chairs à la mandoline. Elegant yet comfortable, a painted and gilded Louis XVI chair with its drapery and fringe à la Pompadour, right, once invited ladies of the court to tarry with a book.

Set between two sumptuously draped living room windows is a handsome three-drawer Louis XIV commode crafted in rosewood by a master ébéniste.

A *Provincial late-18th-century* directoire, *painted gray and up-holstered in deep-green leather,* right, *echoes the colors of a small elegant dining room whose windows open onto a lushly planted courtyard.*

A faience inkwell with a quill pen, above left, *and traveling Sèvres tea set for two,* above right, *are reminders of the gentility of the 18th-century court. A small apartment in Versailles is furnished with this intriguing surprise—a late-18th-century commode with an inlaid-marble trompe l'oeil top depicting a game of cards,* right.

PORCELAIN: SAINT-CLOUD, CHANTILLY, AND SEVRES

Few events had as profound an influence on the development of French decorative arts as the burgeoning of the China trade in the 16th to 17th centuries. Among other sought-after importations were Chinese and Japanese porcelain. Once this hard-glazed ware was introduced to Europe, supply never kept up with demand, and local factories, many founded under royal auspices, began experimenting with ways to reproduce the coveted ware. The porcelain created at the factory in Sèvres was to become one of the most renowned products of France. But earlier efforts created their own distinctive ware, such as soft-paste porcelain, fired at a lower temperature than hard-paste ware. One of the earliest soft-paste wares was developed at Saint-Cloud in the Ile-de-France toward the end of the 17th century, followed by other factories, such as that begun at Chantilly in 1725.

Rare and recherché, *the* pâte-tendre, *or soft-paste, porcelain of Chantilly is known for its predominantly blue patterns on a glowing white ground. Produced from the late 18th century through the late 19th, much of the porcelain of Chantilly,* left and opposite, *as well as that from Saint-Cloud and Sèvres, is distinguished by scalloped borders. Many of the floral motifs were inspired by Oriental porcelain. Other popular motifs were a central carnation, a basketweave pattern, and a fleur-de-lis crown atop the monogram of Louis Philippe.*

POTAGER DU ROY

When it was created at Versailles in the early 1680s under the reign of Louis XIV, the Potager du Roy (the king's vegetable garden) was a magnificent experiment. It remains today one of the most extraordinary gardens in Europe. Open to visitors only by special request, the garden covers 22 impeccably tended acres (8 hectares) several hundred yards south of the palace. Designed and planted by the king's gardener, Jean-Baptiste de la Quintinye, the extensive gardens with a central area divided into 16 equal squares boast exotic varieties of fruits, vegetables, and flowers from around the world. Today the site of France's Ecole Nationale d'Horticulture, the gardens are maintained exactly as they were in the days of Louis XIV.

Under instructions from the enlightened Louis XIV, whose passions included science and engineering, Jean-Baptiste de la Quintinye set out to plant the most unusual vegetable garden in Europe, not only with the widest variety of all plants known to grow in the Ile-de-France climate —peas, lettuce, strawberries, mushrooms, apples, pears—but also with such plants as Louis' beloved figs and melons, native to milder climates. Explorers returning from ventures to North and South America and the Caribbean knew they would please their sovereign by presenting him with botanical offerings. The Potager du Roy evolved into nothing less than the cradle of modern agriculture. La Quintinye's successors, a father and son surnamed Le Normand, even succeeded in cultivating coffee and pineapples in the king's garden. Tall stone walls were built to protect the fruit trees both *en espalier* (against garden walls) and free-growing. Vegetables

The 18th-century Cathédrale Saint-Louis forms an imposing backdrop for the new onions and other vegetables thriving in the carefully tended gardens of Versaille's Potager du Roy, the king's vegetable garden, left. A tall bronze statue of J. B. de la Quintinye, above, surveys the unusual gardens he designed for Louis XIV.

grew in smaller enclosed gardens. The produce from the king's many plots provisioned Versailles, as well as other royal residences, such as Compiègne and the hunting lodges at Fontainebleau.

A green and fertile relic of the 17th century, the Potager du Roy was classified as a *monument historique* in 1926. Under the ministrations of the Ecole Nationale d'Horticulture, the gardens thrive with both ancient plants and new seedlings. Here, along the *allées* where Louis XIV used to stroll with La Quintinye, sturdy centuries-old pear trees stand just across the wall from fragile shoots of a new strain of pea.

A student of the Ecole Nationale d'Horticulture, right, *prepares the soil for a new row of vegetables in one of the many enclosed gardens of the Potager du Roy. Eighteenth-century stone walls cloaked in ivy,* below, *as well as clipped boxwood hedges separate the fruit and vegetable gardens, some of which are reserved for raising produce while others are experimental.*

Each large garden of the Potager is named for a great botanist or for a horticulturist involved over the years with the gardens. The *Jardin Thouin,* left, *is filled with roses and other flowering plants; the* Jardin Legendre, right, *is devoted to espaliered apple trees. Apple trees border a path that leads through the garden,* below, *passing under stone aqueducts designed to carry water to the garden's far reaches.*

MALMAISON

Best known as the home of Josephine de Beauharnais, the Creole first wife of Napoleon Bonaparte, the château of Malmaison is just six miles from Paris in the town of Rueil-Malmaison. A 17th-century structure renovated and embellished with Directoire trappings at the turn of the 19th century, Malmaison, then and now a showcase of Empire style, was Napoleon's favorite residence. He continued to visit there even after his divorce from Josephine, who became chatelaine when they separated in 1809. Napoleon's secretary, Louis Bourrienne, once

Gilded wrought-iron gates, below, *open into Malmaison,* right, *Napoleon and Josephine's Consulate-style château that is distinguished by a perfect symmetry. Today a state-owned museum, Malmaison is a repository of treasures from the Consulate and Empire years.*

stated, "Next to the battlefield, [Malmaison] was the only place where he was truly himself."

Today a state-owned museum, Malmaison houses many works of art and souvenirs from the Empire—the Egyptian expeditions, the European campaigns, even Waterloo. The interior design and furnishings strongly reflect the taste and style of Josephine, who died in 1814. The renowned *tête de sphinx* motifs and swan-neck detailing she loved—symbolic of the Empire—appear in several rooms on chairs and beds. The dining room contains the vermeil service of the city of Paris presented to Napoleon to celebrate his coronation. On the second floor is Josephine's sumptuous bedroom, the Grande Chambre de l'Impératrice, in the shape and style of an oval tent. Portraits of Napoleon, Josephine's Sèvres porcelain services, bronze medallions struck with the Napoleonic image, and even a giant cedar, planted after Napoleon's victory over the Austrians in Marengo, Italy, reflect the brief, lavish, though hardly calm years of Napoleon's Empire.

Set under a leafy arbor on the grounds of Malmaison, the octagonally designed Pavillon d'Eté (Summer Pavilion), above, *was conceived as a cool and elegant warm-weather retreat. The interior décor,* left, *is reminiscent of a sumptuous Moorish tent.*

The oval dining room was designed by the architects Charles Percier and Pierre Fontaine, the team charged with the renovation and furnishing of Malmaison. Faux marbre panels and painted pilasters rise from the dramatic black-and-white diamond floor. Inset between the pilasters is a series of classical trompe l'oeil goddesses painted to resemble bas-reliefs.

Decorated in 1800 by the team of Fontaine and Percier, the library is crowned by an elaborately painted vaulted ceiling, top right, *detailed with garlands, trompe l'oeil architectural detail, and medallions of classical busts and birds. The room is furnished with a collection of handsome Empire fauteuils,* center far right, *some originally from the Tuileries in Paris. A frieze of mythological figures,* bottom far right, *borders a room that was originally Josephine's bathroom. Another classical figure, a graceful goddess,* bottom right, *adorns a wall in the dining room.*

THE PRIX DE DIANE

Every year, on the second Sunday of June, one of the most elegant horse races in the world is run over the elite turf of the Hippodrome de Chantilly—the Chantilly racetrack. In the Prix de Diane, the finest racehorses of Europe circle the course, while lavishly dressed and coiffed spectators cheer from the stands. The four o'clock start permits day-long elegant tailgate lunches and private, tented garden parties, the most elegant hosted by the Hermès company, the venerable

leather goods producer, and the Dumas-Hermès family, the race's sponsors.

To give the Prix de Diane, first run in 1843, added cachet, a different royal lady is invited to preside over the event every year: one year the guest of honor was Princess Anne of England; another year it was Princess Lalla Meryem, daughter of the king of Morocco.

The competition at this festive annual event is fierce both on and off the turf, as *les élégantes* of *le tout Paris* try to outdo one another with their sensational hats, stunning jewels, and one-of-a-kind designer suits.

Ruffles and flourishes, pomp and circumstance characterize the Prix de Diane, the prestigious horse race held annually in June at the Chantilly racetrack. Festivities begin with fanfare and a parade of the elite Garde Républicaine, the palace guard attached to the French head of state, opposite. The race, inaugurated in 1843, is reserved exclusively for three-year-old thoroughbred fillies, which run for the money on a 2,100-meter turf track, right and below.

Peripheral activities, exhibitions, and competitions fill the Sunday of the Prix de Diane in Chantilly. Among the day's events are an exclusive sit-down charity lunch, left, *an antique automobile exhibition,* right, *a picnic, a costume parade, and perhaps the most hotly contested competition of all —the Prix d'Elégance, for which a young woman is selected from the crowd for her elegance and style and awarded a gold Hermès watch.* Overleaf: *a dozen images portray the almost devastating chic of the beau monde who make up the Prix de Diane's inner circle—invited guests of the Hermès company.*

PART TWO
La Vie Artistique
A PAINTER'S IDYLL

An amusing diorama in the Musée de Sceaux, the museum of the history of the Ile-de-France, left, *depicts the frolic and high times of the Impressionist painters, among them Renoir and Monet, who used to gather for reputedly wild weekends at the floating tavern La Grenouillère, moored in Bougival across from Croissy Island. A provincial 19th-century portrait of a noble sheep,* above, *from a home near Dourdan, presents the animal perhaps most symbolic of the Ile-de-France.*

ONE HUNDRED YEARS AFTER THE HEYDAY OF THE IMPRESSIONISTS, ARTISTS AND WRITERS ARE STILL DRAWN TO THE PEACE OF THE ILE-DE-FRANCE COUNTRYSIDE AND THE ROMANTIC LEGENDS OF ITS PAST.

Although the land-scape does not offer the same bounty as the dramatic cliffs of Brittany, the orchards of Normandy, or the light-filled vistas of Provence, the gentle beauty of the Ile-de-France has enchanted many generations of landscape painters. The seminal Barbizon school of painters focused their efforts on depicting the distinctive landscapes and rural life of the region in their large and somewhat somber paintings of the mid-19th century.

Twenty years later the Impressionist movement, with Claude Monet, Alfred Sisley, Johann Jongkind, Camille Pissarro, and Edouard Manet in the avant-garde, blew light and air into their soft-focus landscapes and portraits. Monet installed himself at Giverny; Pissarro and Paul Cézanne set up shop in Pontoise; and Edgar Degas, Auguste Renoir, and Sisley worked in Argenteuil and Louveciennes. Following in their footsteps came André Derain and Maurice de Vlaminck.

The Ile-de-France captured by the Impressionists had a radiant, nostalgic glow. This idealized view of a country idyll still draws Parisians out of the city every weekend.

L'Ancienne Auberge de Père Ganne (The Old Inn of Father Ganne), today a tiny museum in Barbizon, left, *was once the preferred bistro of the Barbizon school artists.* Above, *a painted frieze of classical figures adorns the dining room of Malmaison. A caricature of singer Maurice Chevalier,* above left, *marks the riverside tavern Chez Gégène. An impressionistic view of Giverny,* right, *by a contemporary artist nears completion on the grounds of Monet's former home.*

A PAINTER'S QUARTERS

The old riverside village of Chatou, 10 miles west of Paris along the Seine, is a landmark in the history of art. It was here, in the glory days of Impressionism, that Renoir came to meet the writer Guy de Maupassant for lazy, leisurely lunches at the *guinguettes,* such as La Grenouillère and the Maison Fournaise; and it was here that Renoir captured the spirit of the lively, luminous afternoons in his painting *Le Déjeuner des Canotiers* (*The Boatmen's Lunch;* now in the Phillips Collection, Washington, D.C.). Two decades later, two young painters, André Derain, born in Chatou, and Parisian Maurice de Vlaminck, took the next major step beyond Impressionism toward modern art. Painting in chromatic, almost garish colors with exaggerated or primitive images, they developed a style dubbed Fauvism by a Paris art critic—based on the word *fauve,* meaning wild or wild animal.

In the environment of Chatou's artistic heritage, the young contemporary painter Ramuntcho Barbero de Saint-Amand has chosen a small village apartment, converted from an old estate, as his residence-atelier. Although the proportions are diminutive, the rooms are flooded with color and light. "I was born in Madagascar, and I think the memories of a sun-washed childhood influence the colors and the light I'm drawn to today," says Saint-Amand.

In his small village apartment, the painter Ramuntcho Barbero de Saint-Amand, left, *has created a lively working and residential environment. In his atelier,* right, *bright yellow walls set off his collection of white plaster molds with a classic theme.*

Saint-Amand's rooms are dominated by a golden yellow that warms the interior even on the grayest days. Doors, moldings, and window frames are trimmed with white. A collection of white plaster classical molds—Greek busts, small nudes, and sculptural motifs—enliven the walls, while trompe l'oeil detailing painted by Saint-Amand adds whimsical charm to ceilings and walls. Saint-Amand's impressionistic canvases are casually displayed in his atelier and living room, along with memorabilia from the opera and sculpture of many periods. Frequently animating the rooms is Saint-Amand's large band of friends, who drop in for conversation, advice, or, if they are lucky, one of their host's carefully pre-pared, exotically spiced meals. His quarters may be petite, but his warmth and welcome are grand. "I chose this setting because it's beautiful and practical at the same time," says Saint-Amand, who teaches art in Paris. "It's lush and super-green . . . it was once part of the royal forest of Saint-Germain, and yet it's less than a half hour by train from Paris, where I have another apartment. The Impressionists, who traveled here by train one hundred years ago, found the site as inspiring as I do."

Saint-Amand's diminutive bedroom boasts pieces that might normally furnish a much larger room, such as a canopied brass bed and an imposing sculpture of a female nude, left. *Sculpted busts displayed on pedestals,* right, *dominate the décor in each of the three small rooms.*

A rolltop desk in his atelier keeps Saint-Amand's letters and papers organized and out of sight. The large gilded mirror above the desk reflects the collection of molds on the opposite wall. A simple wood bookcase holds a large collection of art and reference books.

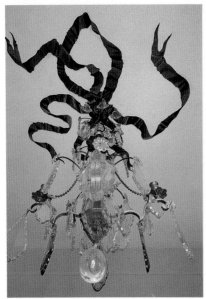

Trompe l'oeil detailing painted by Saint-Amand sets off the crystal chandelier, above, *in the atelier. In the salon a large gilt mirror above the 19th-century buffet infinitely reflects the mirror on the facing wall,* right. *Pastel-striped moiré fabric by Boussac covers the Louis XVI bergère to the right.*

AT THE FOREST'S EDGE

Although they live in Rambouillet, an enviable address, Mireille and Jean-Claude Lothon wanted a simple weekend house with even more of a country atmosphere. They found their small farmhouse, dating from the mid-1700s, only 20 minutes away from their primary residence in a tiny verdant village not far from the edge of the Forest of Rambouillet. As Mireille remembers, "There were very few trees, no flowers, but the setting was there, and the possibilities!"

The house originally had only three rooms, and little exterior light. As with many antique farm-

Although restored, the facade of the 18th-century farmhouse retreat of Jean-Claude and Mireille Lothon has been kept deliberately humble and rustic. Leggy hollyhocks lean across the kitchen door, painted stark white with matching shutters.

98

houses, windows were never an architectural priority—three or four in the house for ventilation and a bit of light, and none so large that they let in the cold air in the winter and the hot air in the summer. The Lothons, like most couples renovating an 18th-century peasant dwelling, had to add windows and skylights to illuminate the somber interior with natural light. To give the living room added volume, they removed the low ceiling and were delighted to discover a network of massive beams under the roof, which they decided to leave exposed. Outside, Mireille planted roses, petunias, geraniums, and daisies in a scattering of rock gardens on the property. Flowers brighten views of the house and from the house at every angle.

The Lothons and their four grown children use the house on every imaginable occasion. Mireille, an artist who took up painting in the late 1970s, is the most frequent resident. It was she who was most involved in the property's metamorphosis from run-down farm to a comfortable and welcoming second home, and it is she who loves it most. "I often come here four or five times a week," says Mireille. "My greatest pleasure here is to paint, outside alone in my garden."

When the Lothons found their long, low weekend house in the 1970s, there were virtually no trees and flowers on the property. But since then, as the views, right, testify, the residence has bloomed under the skillful green thumb of Mireille Lothon, left, at her garden gate, who has planted cherry trees, hydrangeas, roses, petunias, geraniums, daisies, and lavender.

During renovations, the Lothons uncovered the farmhouse's old original beams and decided to leave them exposed. They removed the floor between attic and living room, creating a cathedral ceiling supported by the dramatic old beams.

Furnishings in the living room are homey and unpretentious, drawn from old family furnishings, oversize floor pillows, and Indian fabrics in rose and blue shades, with Mireille Lothon's art on the walls.

The functional, whitewashed kitchen maintains the home's rustic air, with its rough-hewn beams supporting the ceiling and dividing the work area from the dining area. Accent colors of blue and rose brighten the kitchen as they do the adjoining living room.

The entrance hall originally had no window, a very low ceiling, and a beaten-earth floor. The Lothons removed the ceiling to expose the beams, added the mullioned window that looks out on the garden, and installed antique terra-cotta tiling. Mireille Lothon's trompe l'oeil painting propped on the rustic farm table to the right is of the shadows cast by two of the three objects placed in front of it.

IN COLETTE'S SHADOW

The handsome and generously proportioned 17th-century home of Jean-Louis Lécart, mayor of Montfort-l'Amaury, is inhabited by memories of a brilliant past. From the 1920s through the 1940s, the house was the setting for a bucolic, informal literary salon that included some of the leading writers and artists of the day. Germaine de Beaumont, Jean-Louis Lécart's godmother, bought the house in 1910, shortly before she accepted the post of secretary to the French writer Colette, and became part of a coterie of artistic, literary, and musical luminaries that included Jean Cocteau, André Gide, Gertrude Stein and her companion Alice B. Toklas, and the composers Maurice Ravel and Henri Solquet. These celebrated visitors came from Paris, or from their own neighboring Montfort domains, to pass between-the-wars afternoons relaxing in the spacious enclosed garden and engaging in the gentle art of extended conversation. Colette left more than the echoes of her words as a legacy. She gave a full collection of her first editions to Madame de Beaumont, personally

The private face of Jean-Louis Lécart's 17th-century Montfort-l'Amaury home overlooking the back garden, above, *is inset with most of the home's 58 glass doors and windows. Of varying styles and sizes, the apertures include two oeil-de-boeuf windows,* right, *complete with their own tiny half-moon shutters.*

The front entrance to Mayor Lécart's home, hidden behind high stone walls, right, *is flanked by potted hydrangeas and shielded from rain and sun by a cut-metal marquee painted a soft gray-blue to match the shutters and woodwork. The door's glass windows are protected by elaborate wrought-iron grillwork.*

dedicated, and at her death left her friend three of her favorite fauteuils, all part of the current household. Monsieur Lécart also holds, securely locked away, an important collection of unpublished letters from Colette to his godmother. "My house is full of benevolent ghosts," he says. "Everything that I do in this house succeeds."

When Monsieur Lécart inherited the house, on a street running off Montfort's main *place,* he wanted to create a comfortable year-round residence. A career army officer before he became Montfort's busy mayor, he had served as a colonel in Korea, Indochina, and Africa, and then in the Ministry of Foreign Affairs in Paris. He intended to settle down in Montfort, but the house needed major renovation, the mayor recalls. "It was *sans conforts* [without basic amenities]. I had to install electricity and plumbing. Then I took on the exterior facades. There are fifty-eight doors and windows in the house, and most of them

The formal living room is a rich but casual mix of Oriental rugs, antique portraits, engravings, and some furniture that once belonged to the writer Colette and was willed to Lécart's godmother. A small console table on the far wall serves as the bar, while a round table between the French windows displays a collection of crystal paperweights, some also formerly owned by Colette.

needed restoration. While most of the glass is new, there are still some panes over two hundred years old." After the modernization and repair work was complete, it came time to redecorate the house and make it his own.

"I didn't want my home to be a *maison sophistiquée,*" Monsieur Lécart says. "I chose floral-print Laura Ashley wallpaper and fabrics to set the mood; I hung many floral still-life paintings; and I used a lot of green. The salons are a symphony of greens, with every tonality represented, dominated by deep Empire green." Several inherited collections highlight the rooms, including a group of colorful Barbotine faience pieces and a stunning array of antique samplers, one of the best collections in France, hanging in a small pink guest bedroom overlooking the gardens.

A wide, graceful stairway, right, winds up from a stone-tiled foyer to the second-floor salons and bedrooms just visible on the landing. Adorning the curved wall is a collection of antique Japanese prints, left, all set off to advantage against the pale walls in slim red frames.

The ground-floor rooms shown on these pages are decorated in an Empire theme, with many collections displayed throughout. A suite of rooms facing the back garden, *left, is accented in what Lécart calls "Empire green." In the central salon, right, the room with the strongest Empire décor, curtains draping the French doors were created from Laura Ashley fabric. The salon, with several collections of bibelots and family portraits, opens onto the more formal living room,* below right. *The tapestry-covered* fauteuil, below, *is one of several pieces of furniture that originally belonged to the writer Colette.*

In a small guest bedroom with deep rose walls, Lécart displays part of his vast collection of antique needlework, including the pastoral needlepoint scene, left. Samplers of all shapes and sizes, right and below, *were inherited or purchased by Lécart, who continued a collecting passion of his predecessors.*

CHEZ MONET

The flowers of Giverny, their artful disorder conceived by a master, bloom in the colorful display designed by the Impressionist painter Claude Monet in the last years of the 19th century. His celebrated water lilies, immortalized on scores of canvases; the huge willows; the arching trellises of roses; the diminutive green Japanese bridge draped with wisteria; and the winding, densely planted paths are today restored to their original beauty.

Here, roses, acanthus, dahlias, foxgloves, nasturtiums, poppies, pansies, clematis, and tulips are among the countless species of flowers and plants, both annuals and perennials, that grace the gardens bordering the house or fill the Oriental water gardens that stretch out from across a small road that winds through the property. Monet juxtaposed plantings with an artist's eye for colors—marigold and butter yellow, crimson and blush pink, deep purple and lavender. At every step the garden offers an arresting contrast between the vibrant and the gentle. Even more overwhelming to the senses are the perfumes. On a warm, early summer day, the scent of Giverny is paradisiacal.

Monet discovered Giverny, a tiny farm village in the Vexin—a region traversed by the Seine where the Ile-de-France cedes the meadows and pasturelands to Normandy—in the early 1880s, shortly before the lease on his nearby house in Poissy expired. He was immediately captivated by the rambling old pink farmhouse and grounds set at the foot of a hill. He loved the willows and the poplars and the proximity to the Seine, just a few miles away along the Epte, a tiny tributary that flows through the town. Monet moved to Giverny in 1883 at the age of 43, along with Alice Hoschedé, his mistress and later second wife, his

Monet was instantly captivated by the pink farmhouse he spotted from a train in the early 1880s, top. *The pink, green, and white facade, seen here behind the trellised portico in full summer bloom, serves as a backdrop for the gardens that stretch out from the bottom of the green steps, and in which lushly blooming flowers in variegated pinks,* above, *predominate.*

Garlanded in wisteria, Monet's renowned Japanese bridge, left, *which he had built in 1895, arches over the pond in the lower garden, once again planted with water lilies. From a distant perspective, the bridge,* right, *is in perfect harmony with the imaginative spectrum of irises, lilies, climbing roses, and willows.*

Claude Monet's house, almost an icon among art historians as well as a popular destination for tourists, is surprising in its simplicity and endearing in its hominess. More than six decades after Monet's death at Giverny in 1926, the house still projects the sense of a full life richly lived. Restored at the end of the 1970s under the supervision of Gérard van der Kemp, the restorer and curator of the palace of Versailles, the home is a re-creation of the way Monet lived, with the choice of colors and furnishings as accurate as a careful perusal of Monet's correspondence and notebooks and many old photographs could make it.

The exterior of the long, two-story, pink-and-green farmhouse is painted in colors derived from the hues of Monet's garden, the

sons Jean and Michel, and Alice's six children. Here, he set out to establish the tranquil, comfortable home that had eluded him for so many years, a place where he could live happily with his large family, entertain, and above all paint.

The gardens captured Monet's attention almost from the beginning, and he devoted the hours when he was not painting to planning, puttering, and planting. In the late 1880s, the financial insecurity that had haunted Monet for most of his life dissipated as he finally attained recognition as a major artist. After decades of frustration, his paintings not only began to sell, but commanded high prices; collectors sought him out. In 1890 Monet was able to buy the home in Giverny, which he had been renting, and he began to devote himself to his gardens with an even greater fervor, enlarging the array of the plantings, adding clusters of bamboo trees and new roses to the Oriental garden, and expanding the pond.

Giverny today, in addition to being a museum open to the public, is used for many private receptions and dinners. Here caterers prepare the front terrace for an afternoon tea for a visiting group of art aficionados.

soft pink echoing the trellised roses, the myrtle green of the shutters and doors repeating the shade of the trellises themselves. Within the house, each room has its own color scheme, with greens, blues, and yellows dominating.

The most celebrated room is the low, luminous yellow dining room on the first floor, set between the foyer and the kitchen. The dining room walls are actually three subtle shades of yellow: canary, citron, and jonquil. The cabinets and armoires are also painted yellow in a monochromatic scheme inspired by artist James Whistler's apartment in Paris. Photographs of the room in Monet's day show chairs with caned seats. Today, blue plaid tie-on cushions add a note of color to the painted Louis XVI–style provincial chairs. A collection of Japanese prints, a display of blue-and-white export porcelain, a red-and-cream tile floor, and tall green vases holding bouquets of lilies, begonias, and orchids set the mood of the simple room. Monet loved cut flowers and had large bouquets brought in from the garden to brighten up the interior on rainy days.

Many contemporary artists come to work at Giverny, left, *as much of a paradise for painters today as it was in Monet's time when friends like Whistler, Manet, and Renoir came to capture their impressions of the gardens on canvas. In his gardens,* right, *Monet juxtaposed colors and textures the way he did on canvas.* Preceding pages: *impressions of Giverny.*

Japanese prints, Chinese porcelain, exotic *objets,* and of course the beguiling Oriental garden reflect Monet's lifelong passion for the subtle, sophisticated, and deceptively simple art of the Orient, particularly Japan. An avid collector of the works of such Japanese artists as Hokusai and Utamaro, he was 16 when he bought his first Japanese print, of parakeets and monkeys, in Le Havre for just a few francs. The brilliant colors and refined, stylized technique of the print made a lasting impression on him. During a trip to Amsterdam in 1871, at the age of 30, Monet spotted a large collection of Japanese prints in a shop where he was negotiating the purchase of a blue-and-white pitcher. The dealer threw them in for the pitcher's asking price. Some of these are among the 300 prints that hang throughout Giverny today.

The large kitchen, where Alice Monet prepared woodcock and

In the dazzling monochromatic dining room, left, *walls, ceilings, and furniture are all painted in hues of yellow. Surrounding the table that accommodates 14 is a set of Louis XVI–style provincial cane-seated chairs. Some of the Japanese figurative prints from Monet's vast collection cover the walls in simple wood frames. French, Dutch, and Chinese ceramic platters add color and contrast on the walls between the two cabinets,* above. *On the table in the foreground is the famous "Giverny plate," part of a porcelain service created in Marly that repeats the yellow-and-blue theme of the room. The rich yellow room glows in dramatic contrast to the adjoining kitchen,* top.

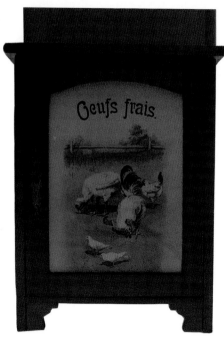

Echoing the kitchen's blue-and-white theme, a small ceramic and wood egg cabinet is mounted between the windows in the foyer.

her favorite rhubarb pie for the many guests that passed through Giverny, is a symphony of blues. The walls and ceiling are in two tones of blue, matched by the cabinets and tables. Blue-and-white faience tiles in assorted patterns cover the walls from floor to ceiling. The only contrast comes from the red hexagonal tiles of the floor, and the gleaming copper pots hanging from the walls.

On the opposite side of the foyer from the dining room, beyond a small blue anteroom, is the sitting room that Monet called his atelier, a spacious, airy salon where the family gathered in the evenings to listen to Monet read aloud. On the walls three tiers of unframed canvases represented Monet's work at several periods of his career. Today the room is filled with reproductions; there are, in fact, no original Monet paintings at Giverny.

Upstairs, Monet's large light-washed bedroom is a restful cream and white, with lace-covered bed and lace curtains. The tall double windows, where each morning at dawn Monet checked the day's weather, open onto the kaleidoscopic gardens below. Madame Monet's much more modest bedroom, adjoined to Monet's by a long foyer, is a pale green with blue borders and is decorated with the ubiquitous Japanese prints. The armoire and bedstead are in polished woods,

Tiled in an assortment of blue-and-white faience squares, the kitchen, with its blue table and checked curtains, is enhanced by a large period stove and a gleaming collection of copper pots, pans, and pitchers.

The walls of Madame Monet's modest bedroom, *above* and *right, are painted in muted shades of blue and green and decorated with more of Monet's collection of Japanese prints, as is an adjoining foyer, top, used as a washroom, that links Madame's bedroom with that of her husband.*

among the very few pieces of unpainted furniture at Giverny.

Monet lived 43 years, exactly half his life, at Giverny. After he died, in 1926, the house's chief resident was his step-daughter (and daughter-in-law) Blanche, also a painter. At Blanche's death in 1940, the house remained in the family but was no longer inhabited. Over the decades it grew derelict, the gardens wild, tangled, and choked. Monet's younger son, Michel, bequeathed the property at his death in 1966 to the Académie des Beaux-Arts, in the hope that one day the property would be restored as a tribute and memorial to his father. Gérard van der Kemp took on the project in 1977. After three years of exhaustive research and meticulous restoration, aided by Van der Kemp's American wife, Florence, and with donations from benefactors on both sides of the Atlantic, the gardens and the house, christened the Musée Claude Monet, opened to the public in the spring of 1980. Giverny is one of France's special places, a unique and once again thriving environment that is a living testament to the life and genius of Claude Monet.

The master bedroom of Claude Monet is the least colorful, most subdued room in his house. The restful color scheme of cream and white is accented by both painted and unpainted furniture, a large mirror, and a collection of family photographs. From his windows he could overlook his gardens.

A PLAYWRIGHT'S HAVEN

When the author of the play *Boeing-Boeing* (premiered on Broadway in the winter of 1965) and the manager of Paris's Théâtre Michel want to escape the rigors and demands, public and private, of the theatrical world, they head for their tall 18th-century house secure behind high white walls in the town of Montfort l'Amaury. Here playwright Marc Camoletti and his wife, Germaine, enjoy a rare luxury in modern times—privacy without isolation.

Montfort l'Amaury is a fashionable and expensively restored town 15 minutes west of Versailles, with cobbled streets, antique street lanterns, a Gothic cloister, and many weekend homes sheltering celebrities and aristocrats from Paris. Many of the discreetly walled homes in town, including the Camolettis', enclose jewel-like gardens invisible from the road. The Camolettis bought their house, built in 1763, in the early 1970s, before Montfort became superchic. (The town has been quietly à la mode since the 1920s.) "I always loved Montfort,"

Playwright Marc Camoletti and his wife, Germaine, a theater manager, above, *relax in their walled garden during a weekend break from the Paris theater. Displayed atop a piano in a small salon,* right, *are portraits of the Camolettis painted shortly after their marriage by Marc Camoletti's father. The small, discreet entrance to the Camolettis' home on a side street in Montfort-l'Amaury,* far right, *is bordered in vines.*

says Germaine. "When it came time to look for a second home, we looked here. When we found this house it was in a derelict condition. Dust and spiders and water and filth were everywhere. One has to have a lot of imagination and faith to undertake the renovation of a house in such condition!"

The décor chez Camoletti is stylish and plush, with such accoutrements as heavy silk damask curtains, a canopied canapé (daybed), and white silk upholstery on the living room sofa and chairs. The house is elegant by day, but it comes to life at night, when the interior warms with the illumination of candles and the many striking lamps and sconce lights. In fact, it was designed with an after-dark lifestyle in mind. "We're night people," Germaine says, "and this is a house that lives at night."

In the foyer of the Camolettis' home, an upholstered fauteuil flanks a round, draped lamp table clustered with potted hydrangeas, a bowl of fresh cherries, and assorted bibelots. The house portrait on the wall behind the lamp is by Marc Camoletti.

Blue-and-white Italian tilework enhances the walls of the Camolettis' rustic, beamed kitchen, right, *where an old farm table functions as a worktable. A quaint touch of color is added by a small reproduction of a Vermeer,* below, *displayed over a countertop.*

A handsome wrought-iron railing, installed by the Camolettis during their renovation, leads up the carpeted stairway to the second floor. An unusual chandelier of glass and wrought iron illuminates the stairway.

Invisible from the street, the Camolettis' home is reached through a doorway set into the thick ivy-covered walls, left, *to the front garden. The flying buttresses of the 18th-century Eglise Saint-Pierre soar above the walls of the Camolettis' back garden,* above.

In a corner of the garden, left, *a
small tile-roofed "shed" with a
mullioned door is a charming
receptacle for gardening implements and lawn furniture. Awaiting cocktail guests early on a
summer's eve is a set of white
wrought-iron park chairs and
stools around a table,* above.

ESTATE OF GRACE

Off a country road in Chatou, close to the Seine, an elegant, tree-shaded estate dating from the 18th century exudes an air of profound harmony and calm. The scent of honeysuckle sweetens the ambiance of this ivy-covered domain belonging to a distinguished literary family. Within the house order prevails. A graceful series of rooms leads the visitor through the understated interiors in an almost organic progression. The furnishings, many from the 18th century, complement the subtly molded walls and marble-tiled floors.

In a setting that would have inspired Renoir, nature adds its own artful strokes of color and texture to the property. An *allée* of linden trees stretches out from the kitchen door, while a bower of tea roses in the garden, heavy with blossoms and the perfume of happy memories, longs to be picked. Oaks and willows shade the soft green lawn below the house's tall French windows that bathe the interior in natural light. There is a striking rapport between interior and exterior elements of this home just minutes from Paris that is more often seen in the fine homes of Provence. Vases, urns, and faience bowls hold bountiful bouquets or mounds of dried blossoms from the gardens; lush green views impose themselves upon the rooms from every window. And truly bringing the outside in—or the inside out—is a remarkable trompe l'oeil mural by the artist Ramuntcho Barbero de Saint-Amand in the game room that portrays the gardens just outside the door across a wall flanking the Ping-Pong table.

A dense, leafy archway of chestnut trees at the wrought-iron gates, left, *leads into the graveled courtyard of a country estate in the town of Chatou, west of Paris. A thick blanket of ivy surrounds the tall French windows,* above, *which illuminate the high-ceilinged rooms of the second floor that overlook the back garden.*

An assortment of soberly upholstered Louis XV fauteuils in a salon is arranged before an elegantly sculpted 18th-century mantelpiece. The bookshelves to the right of the fireplace are inset beneath a narrow stairway enclosed by sensuous ironwork.

Carved molding, contrast-painted in white, gives definition and charm to bookshelves and cabinets built into the library wall. The contemporary sofa and two matching armchairs are slip-covered in gunmetal-blue velour.

A paradigm of elegance and simplicity, the luminous white dining room shows to advantage the graceful early 19th-century English library table, now used for dining, and late 18th-century Sheraton chairs. Two glass-paned doors lead into the marble-tiled room, balanced, on the opposite wall, by built-in display cabinets on either side of the 18th-century mantelpiece.

In the foyer beyond the dining room illuminated by an 18th-century wrought-iron lantern, a romantic 19th-century cast-bronze sculpture sits atop an un-usual late 19th-century Italian buffet cabinet with mirrored sides and top, accented by trompe l'oeil–painted wood detailing.

Across from the mirrored buffet in the foyer, a 19th-century Dutch landscape mural serves as a backdrop for a late 18th-century Sheraton half-moon table holding a striking late-19th-century French faience bowl full of fragrant dried rose petals from the garden.

PART THREE

Villes et Villages

LIFE IN TOWN

A winding rural road, the D11, or départementale 11, passes peaceful villages such as Courgent, left, along the way. On the morning of May 1, every village square fills with amateur vendors, above, selling bunches of lilies of the valley, the day's traditional flower and a portent of good luck.

PARIS AND HER ATTRACTIONS MAY BE ONLY A FEW MILES AWAY, BUT FOR THOSE WHO LIVE IN THE ILE-DE-FRANCE, THE UNIVERSE IS CENTERED IN THEIR OWN IDYLLIC VILLAGE, TOWN, OR HAMLET.

Each of the small, traditional towns and villages scattered throughout the Ile-de-France is a hub around which radiates the rural life of the region. The classic Ile-de-France village has a small *place* (town square) dominated by a solid old stone church and surrounded by *tilleuls taillés* (pruned linden trees). A *boulangerie,* a café, and a grocery store/butcher shop are sometimes the only businesses; in very tiny communities, one establishment sometimes fills all three functions.

Village dwellers live on the *place,* or on the small streets that lead off from the center, in 17th-, 18th-, or 19th-century houses. Small, neat, and more symmetrical than their rural farm neighbors, the village houses characteristically include dormer windows, sometimes gables, and steep roofs generally of sleek terra-cotta tiles.

Many towns in the Ile-de-France have weekly open markets, with stands of the freshest meat, vegetables, and flowers. Here prince and peasant rub shoulders and swap quips while haggling over the price of tomatoes. Many towns also sponsor an annual fair or festival to celebrate a local product or event.

The small, ornate train station in Senlis, left, bears a plaque reading: "This station was built in 1922 in place of the one that the Germans burned down on September 2, 1914." A painting in the Musée de Sceaux portrays servants at work in the interior courtyard of a château in the Ile-de-France, above left. Two children, above, buy a nosegay of lilies of the valley for their mother on May 1. The plats du jour *are listed on the window of a village bistro, right. Overleaf: A mosaic of rustic facades from the four corners of the Ile-de-France reveals both the harmony and charm of regional design, as well as the diversity of local style.*

LIVING ON THE GREEN

While her family and friends continue to reside in Paris, Geneviève Prou, a woman "of a certain age" who moved away from the capital several years ago, prefers her home in a little village at the southern reaches of the Ile-de-France, with one of everything: one *boulangerie,* one pharmacy, one hotel, one antiques dealer, and one church. From her house facing the village's small green, she can view almost all of these enterprises, as well as the church, at a glance. Her home's diminutive facade, so small and perfect it resembles a dollhouse observed from the green, belies the comfortably proportioned house and spacious garden behind.

As if recalling the first encounter with a future lover, the owner vividly remembers her first viewing of the 18th-century town house while making rounds with a real estate agent. "We arrived at the house at seven o'clock in the evening," she relates. "The bells from the church began ringing. I took one look at the house and I said, 'I'll take it.' "

Impeccably maintained, Geneviève Prou's 18th-century maisonette, above right, *presents a prim, pristine facade to the world passing along her small village's main street, while the private rear facade,* left, *is more sensuous, vibrant, and romantic. Madame Prou,* right, *often receives visits from the neighborhood children. A lion's-head grotesque door knocker,* far right, *announces arrivals.*

The owner's training at the Ecole d'Art-Déco in Paris during her student years, as well as an innate flair for the use of color to enhance the function of every room, is apparent throughout the house. The foyer, covered in golden yellow fabric, leads into the peaceful living room painted in celadon green. Giving onto the living room is the cheerful saffron dining room, which in turn leads down three steps to the blue-and-white kitchen. Upstairs the same sensitivity to color prevails, with rose, soft green, apricot, and pale yellow—the colors of a spring garden—defining the bedrooms. Each room has a share of the owner's carefully chosen collection of antiques gathered over a lifetime. ("I have always loved *objets* and old things," she declares.) Perhaps more than anything else, what unifies the decorative scheme of each room are handsome, vibrant cotton prints, most by Pierre Frey, Madame Prou's former husband, or their son Patrick Frey, that adorn the windows, upholster the furniture, cover the bedding, and border the walls throughout the house.

A cut-velvet upholstered canapé between the living room windows is made more comfortable by the addition of a long tapestry bolster. The canapé pitched its sitters forward until Madame Prou shortened its back legs. ("My guests used to complain that I had arranged it," recalls Madame Prou, "so that nobody would sit too long!")

The large garden behind the house, complete with an antique "summer house" for outdoor dining, reflects the color and floral themes of the interior. Roses, peonies, lavender, and potted geraniums bloom profusely around the edge of the house, along the bricked path, and across the weathered brown walls of the summer house. Set between the house and the summer house is the leafy *potager,* surrounded, in the classic French manner, with a floral border. Finally, behind the summer house is a thick green lawn shaded by fruit trees.

At a white wrought-iron garden table, a vantage point for surveying the splendors of her plantings, the owner likes to receive neighborhood children who frequently drop by for conversation and a sweet. Here too she plays bridge, has dinner parties, and entertains her three sons, seven grandchildren, and one great-grandchild who journey from Paris to visit *grandmère* on weekends and holidays. "For myself, I am perfectly happy to stay here in my village," she says. "I go into Paris as little as possible. . . . I don't want to become crazy like the others!"

Among the room's distinctive collectibles is the voluminously proportioned varnished wicker basket holding bunches of glass grapes and a variety of wax fruits.

153

One of the living room's most striking features is its antique boiserie. Madame Prou left her home's beams exposed, painting them white with a soft yellow between the beams. "My family and friends tell me beams aren't chic any more, but I like them," she says.

A downstairs guest bedroom has an eclectic mix of furnishings that includes a Louis XVI bed, a Lloyd Loom wicker chair, and chintz floral fabric by Pierre Frey. The portrait above the bed, a favorite of Madame Prou's, is one of the first antiques she ever purchased.

The rich yellow fabric walls of the foyer form a backdrop for a 19th-century marquetry commode topped by a dramatic floral still life.

A Lloyd Loom chair in the corner of the living room, right, *has been painted in a butterscotch shade to match the curtain covering the entrance to the kitchen. A generous Louis XV bergère upholstered in a Pierre Frey floral print sits beside the living room's graceful sculpted stone fireplace of the same period,* below right.

Subtly influenced by the dining room at Giverny, Madame Prou chose the same Louis XVI–style side chairs, painted a soft yellow, for her dining room table that encircle the large table at Monet's residence. Above the dining table is a painted 19th-century birdcage, a stylish conceit currently fashionable in elegant French country homes.

The enchanting back garden includes a graveled pathway through the potager, *leading to the trellised flagstone patio where Madame Prou frequently entertains her guests in the summer. Just beyond the ivy-covered walls and tiled roofs of the house hovers the steeple of the village church.*

The small kitchen, three steps down from the living room and opening onto the back garden, is emphatically blue and white, from its painted beams to the faience tiles to the blue-trimmed white cabinet doors. Part of Madame Prou's large collection of baskets is suspended from the beams.

For her master bedroom under the eaves Madame Prou chose the soft fresh colors of a spring garden. The rose hue of the walls is embellished by floral print borders at the ceiling, along the floor, at corners, and around doorways. The floral window fabric is by Pierre Frey. Practical indoor-outdoor carpeting covers the floor.

A Chinese porcelain urn holding a pot of brilliant magenta petunias is a dramatic counterpoint to the stone and terra-cotta brick that defines most of the garden.

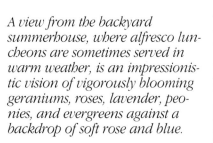

A view from the backyard summerhouse, where alfresco luncheons are sometimes served in warm weather, is an impressionistic vision of vigorously blooming geraniums, roses, lavender, peonies, and evergreens against a backdrop of soft rose and blue.

LES ETOURNELLES

In a tiny village several miles north of Chantilly, the property of an ancient farm that traces its roots back to 51 B.C. dominates the rustic community today, much as it has since the Middle Ages. Large iron gates on the village's main street open onto the large courtyard that fronts the property's early 18th-century *maison de maître,* or master's house; at the side the bell towers of the village church loom above the far wall of the huge *potager.* The town apparently grew up around the farm between 1637 and 1848, the two centuries when it was a thriving agricultural estate, belonging first to a succession of nobles and then passing into the hands of one of its tenant farmers, Antoine Boucher, in 1795, who acquired it from entrepreneurs after the Revolution.

In 1848 Les Etournelles farm underwent a profound transformation in character. With the mar-riage of Augustine Boucher, the farmer's granddaughter, to Eugène Leclerc, the property was converted from a working farm into a comfortable bourgeois residence with five acres of English gardens, a rambling, bucolic style of landscaping fashionable in mid-19th-century France. Les Etournelles grew more grand, more sophisticated. It was during this epoch, when the true farming ceased, that the impressive and fashionable *potager* was designed and planted.

Direct descendants of Antoine Boucher currently inhabit the farm. Parisians by necessity, the couple nevertheless spends at least six months of the year here, an hour north of Paris. Married on the neatly landscaped grounds— little changed from the English gardens planted in 1848—shortly after World War II, they have a

Once the hub of a thriving agricultural estate, the stone "master's house" overlooking a paved courtyard, above, *is the country home of a family descended from the post-Revolutionary owner. An elaborate and carefully tended* potager *surrounded by walls,* right, *retains the same design it had when it was planted in the mid-1800s.*

strong affection for Les Etournelles. The family heirlooms that
fill the house come mostly from
the region, including a Restoration table in the library, Creil faience, a collection of copperware,
and a generous Restoration bathtub, dating from 1848, in the master bedroom.

The couple's seven children and
17 grandchildren seem to share
the owners' devotion to the house
and the land. Family weddings
continue to take place here, as do
other major events and most holidays. Les Etournelles has even inspired one son to take up the toil
of a *cultivateur:* after 150 fallow
years, the property has once again
become a working farm, with 100
apple trees, 60 pear trees, and 20
cherry trees.

A gardener's shed, left, *just outside
the walls of the* potager *is niched
in the corner of a small fenced
garden across from the main
house. In the pastiche of property
views,* right, *fresh spring blossoms
only weeks old are juxtaposed
with architectural elements such
as the tiled barn roof with its rustic dovecote and the simple oeil-
de-boeuf window in the barn's facade that have survived a revolution and two world wars.*

169

The informal salon off the foyer, hung with family portraits, seats family and friends on a variety of 18th- and 19th-century fauteuils, some upholstered with tapestry. The firescreen is a tapestry stitched with the letter B for the Boucher family.

In the living room, a provincial sculpted Regency game table displays a 19th-century soupière (tureen) from Nevers, with a distinctive vegetable theme.

In the formal living room walls are adorned, alternately, with elegant 18th-century gilded pillar appliqués and naïve 18th-century oil-on-canvas panels, here encompassing a door. In front of a Louis XV side table is a rustic 19th-century banquette for two.

In the mustard-yellow biblio-thèque, right, off the formal living room, the room's paneling is high-lighted with terra-cotta–toned trim. A simple Restoration table in the center of the room holds 19th-century Creil bowls and an antiquarian botanical guide, in closeup, above.

A *mélange of terra-cotta tiles, old wood paneling, antique copper, and saffron walls creates the kitchen's warm, burnished glow,* left. *The 16th-century Louis XIII chest carved in oak displays lilacs from the garden. The 19th-century faience bowl,* below, *was manu-factured in the town of Creil. The unusual inlaid oak kitchen table,* right, *was custom-made for the family in Rennes in 1925.*

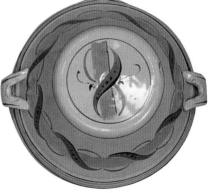

Dominating the master bathroom is a large Louis Philippe zinc bathtub dating from 1848. The late-19th-century swan-head faucets were purchased at auction at the Hôtel Drouot in Paris. To the right of the tub is a Louis XV-style closestool (indoor latrine) with a hinged caned seat.

In a small guest bedroom, left, a ruffled bassinet awaits the visit of the newest grandchild. The Restoration period of Louis Philippe defines the master bedroom, right, with its marble-topped dresser and highboy, sleekly styled tapestry chairs, and collection of period engravings on the wall.

TO MARKET

Thursday is market day in Milly-la-Forêt. Just after dawn the ancient *halles,* the town's unique covered market halls built of oak and chestnut in 1479, begin to fill with vendors. By nine o'clock, the *halles* buzz with activity; shoppers from Milly and the countryside are joined by those who drive in from the nearby towns of Courances, Fleury-en-Bière, and la Ferté-Alais, as well as tourists who make the excursion to see the old *halles* in action. Meats, poultry, dairy goods, and produce sold at the individual stands come from all over France, but the featured items are those produced locally in the Ile-de-France: *fraises des bois,* tiny perfumed wild strawberries abundant in June and July; the cheeses Coulommiers and Brie, the latter described by the Duke of Talleyrand as "the king of cheeses"; summer raspberries; tiny *champignons de Paris;* blackberries in August and September; fresh chestnuts in October; and the *poules d'Houdan,* the meaty, delicately flavored hens of Houdan and their eggs.

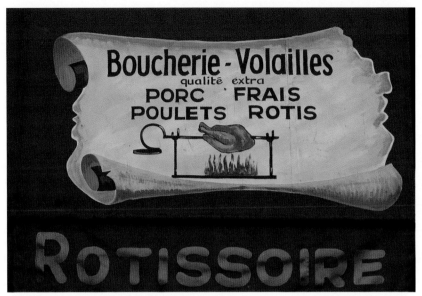

Thursday is Market Day in Milly-la-Forêt. *Just after dawn the stalls sheltered beneath the town's 15th-century covered marketplace begin to fill with produce, cheeses, poultry, meats, and bread. A carved symbol of the French Republic,* far left, *adorns the beams of the old halles. The market is in full swing,* left, *at 10 A.M. Top left, a butcher's sign announces fresh and roasted chicken and pork. Just outside the market, set in the* centre ville, *signs indicate the way to nearby towns and the city of Orléans, farther south,* above.

A farmer sells his fruit under a striped awning, *top right. In an adjacent hall,* above, *dry goods are offered at bargain prices. At the close of Market Day, empty wooden crates,* right, *are stacked on the curb awaiting a return to the farm. Left, an old wall painting advertises a mint liqueur, Millymenthe, once produced in the town.*

179

BEYOND TOWN WALLS

High stone walls rising above a narrow side street in Fontainebleau enclose an estate so quiet and serene that it could well sit deep in the provincial countryside rather than in a town of 20,000 inhabitants that receives nearly 1 million visitors a year. The walls and the greenery seem to shut out all the sounds of a thriving tourist town—cars, buses, and high-voltage, high-pitched voices of countless school groups. In the garden of the *potager*—itself walled to conceal the vegetables from the main house—you can almost hear the green beans growing.

There are actually two houses within this unusual property: the main house built in the early 1800s and inset with striking terra-cotta cartouches—a specialty of Fontainebleau—around the facade; and a guesthouse next door, a slightly smaller replica of the main house built by the home's previous owners in 1921. The guesthouse overlooks the *potager,* while the main house surveys a broad green lawn and the graveled drive lined with flowers.

The current owners, an esteemed French general and his gracious wife, have lived in the home for less than two decades, but have so imbued the property with their character and style that it appears always to have been in the same family since its construction in 1815. The *potager* is 100 years old, with gnarled, thick-limbed miniature apple trees that bear witness to its 19th-century origins, yet the annuals, perennials, and fruit trees, all planted by the owners, look as comfortably established as the *potager.* With flowers and trees, the owners wanted to enhance the impression of being deep in the countryside.

In the center of Fontainebleau, an elegant early 19th-century château, is an island of calm surrounded by broad lawns and protected by tall stone walls. Terra-cotta cartouches, created in Fontainebleau and installed above the first-floor windows, add a distinctive touch to the sober, understated design.

When the general and his wife
purchased the property from an
American couple who had resided
there for 45 years, they embarked
on extensive interior renovations.
They painted or covered the walls
with handsomely printed papers,
and had living room furniture upholstered in richly colored Oriental floral prints in ruby and
sapphire tones from the houses of
Boussac and Braquenié, with
curtains to match. Several small
pieces of painted furniture—a
tapestry-cushioned fauteuil, a
"duchesse"-style chaise longue
with brocade pillows—could de-

*A portrait of the general's Ameri-
can grandmother as a young girl
in Louisiana dominates the stairway leading from the entry hall to
the second floor,* right. *In a corner of the entry,* below, *an antique barometer still gives an
accurate reading of the weather.*

fine the 18th-century Ile-de-France provincial style with their charm and sophistication. As with many warm and gracious French homes, the house projects a sense of family and roots, of generations past that are still somehow present. Dominating the wall of the graceful stairway that winds up from the foyer, a portrait of the general's American grandmother as a little girl in antebellum Louisiana is a smiling testimony to family ties that extend across cultures, centuries, and the Atlantic Ocean.

Rose walls, as well as a black marble fireplace, add warmth to a small study off the living room. Pinstripes in the fabric on the Louis XVI fauteuil pick up the color of the walls.

On the living room's marble mantelpiece an intricately worked late-18th-century clock is flanked by elaborate candelabra and reflected in a large 19th-century gilt mirror.

A collection of family souvenirs, left, *adorns a wide table backing one of the living room's several sofas. Jewel-toned fabrics from the Paris houses of Braquenié and Boussac fill the harmoniously proportioned living room,* right.

A directoire *theme predominates in the general's bedroom, from the color and print of the toile de Jouy fabric of the curtains and walls to the furnishings, which include an elegant fauteuil and a portrait of Napoleon above the desk.*

The ocher hue of the walls, curtains, and bedspread enhances the stylish, masculine ambiance of the general's bedroom, left. A fine example of decorating on a theme, the room has a harmony and purity that reflect a single, short stylistic period at the end of the 18th and beginning of the 19th centuries. Below left, a small antechamber off the bedroom is used as a dressing room.

The general's bathroom, with its faux marbre walls, moody, romantic etchings, and side chair covered in toile de Jouy, continues the directoire theme of the bedroom.

A guesthouse, left, on the grounds of the château, is a small-scale replica of the main house, constructed by the property's former American owners in 1921. Stretching out from the front of the guesthouse is the potager, below right and left, planted a century ago with venerable apple trees espaliered to border the garden. The flowering shrubs and flowers that line the gravel path along the main lawn, right, were planted by the current owners.

THE FAIENCE OF CREIL

The town of Creil-sur-Oise, today a small industrial town in the Oise *département* in the northern Ile-de-France near Senlis, made a permanent name for itself in the early 19th century when a local *manufacture* began producing opaque porcelain and faience with distinctive representational black or gray designs. The Manufacture de Creil was founded on the Oise River in 1797 by Robert Bray O'Reilly, a Paris crystal producer, and was acquired by Charles Alexandre Saint-Cricq in 1816. Three important faience designers established the Creil style: Antoine Legros d'Anizy, Jean Hurford Stone, and Marie Martin Athanase Coquerel. The most characteristic of the production are the sets of bright mustard-yellow plates (it was the clay itself that was tinted yellow) with black transfer patterns depicting elegant ladies and gentlemen, pastoral landscapes, and scenes of town life. Other decorative themes included religion, geography, botany, Italian architectural ruins, scenes of ancient Rome, hunting scenes, and rural mother-and-child depictions. So elaborate were some displays that Creil faience is sometimes referred to as a precursor of the comic strip.

Made at the Montereau Creil factory, the sugar bowl, left, has a lively polychromed pastoral scene complete with a peasant couple on the lid and reclining cow on the bowl. Glazed in the distinctive Creil yellow, the pieces from an earthenware set, right, are a teacup, a soup cup, and a sugar bowl, with a unique ropelike decoration called décor de cordages. *All were made about 1830, and photographed in the Musée de Sceaux.*

A charming product of the Creil factory between 1825 and 1833 was the rebus plate, left. *A rebus conveys a clever aphorism through a riddle of words, letters, and pictures. Far more common was the* soupière, right, *here with a figure holding a trident.*

Various scenes of village life enliven a two-handled soup cup fitted with a cover to keep the contents hot.

In a form more frequently seen in silver, a pedestaled coffeepot has an attractive decorative theme of plants and a bird with open beak as a spout.

Each hand-painted piece of this demitasse set features a slightly different pastoral view—each idyllically portrayed.

MONSIEUR GOSSELIN'S DREAM HOUSE

Destiny, says Jean-François Gosselin, led him to find, and ultimately to buy, his antique home in the center of Montfort-l'Amaury. "I had been living in a small house in a village called Richebourg, near Houdan, and I decided I wanted a home that was larger and more 'noble,'" he relates. "Through an agency I went to see this house first, and it was a *'coup de foudre'*—love at first sight! It was the only one I saw—I never looked at another. To find this house in the town of Montfort—for me the most ravishing village in the Ile-de-France, beautiful in every season—was like a dream. But after I found it, I couldn't buy it until I had sold my other house. It took a full year to find a buyer in Richebourg. But the house in Montfort was still waiting for me, and I knew then that I had been destined to buy it."

Gosselin's spacious and elegant three-story home was one of several in Montfort built in the 18th century when the town was still the administrative seat for the region, a function assumed by Rambouillet in the 19th century. Grand and bourgeois, with tall windows and a steep tiled roof, the house was most likely constructed by one of the high officials in the local government. Originally the house was surrounded by a vast park that was subdivided over time; a large section is today the domain of the Ecole Saint-Louis, an elite boarding school.

One of the aspects of the house that first beguiled Gosselin was

Enclosed by a wall, the paved 18th-century courtyard of Jean-François Gosselin's home in Montfort-l'Amaury, above, *is enlivened by an array of potted plants and wrought-iron park furniture. In the living room,* right, *a mélange of family heirlooms and acquired antiques creates a warm,* sympathique *ambiance. The curtain fabric on the French doors and windows is by Boussac.*

the large, original 18th-century cobblestone courtyard lush with old climbing roses clinging to the stone walls. After he became master of the house, Mr. Gosselin further embellished the courtyard with boxwoods clipped into spiral or ball topiary, wisteria, rhododendrons, and hydrangeas.

While he functioned as gardener for the exterior of his house, Gosselin, an antiques dealer with a stand at the Paris Marché des Puces, acted as his own decorator for the interior. "In decorating, I aimed to create a harmony of warm colors, and to give a sense of space as well as a sense of well-being. I chose large, welcoming sofas and an eclectic mix of old

In the dining room, left and above, *the table, covered in a 19th-century* cachemire *(a woven shawl from Kashmir), is surrounded by a set of provincial Louis XVI chairs with a Montgolfier, or hot-air-balloon, design. The richly patinated antique* buffet à deux-corps *was crafted in the Ile-de-France. On the second floor,* below, *a long, luminous gallery leads to the bedrooms.*

pieces of varying styles and periods to give the impression of an old *maison de famille*—a home that had been in the family a long, long time." Many of the antiques furnishing his home are family heirlooms. Others were acquired here and there over the years. Because of his métier as an antiques dealer, Gosselin notes, he has been able to compile a list of many fine and special sources, and from each one of them he's tried to keep at least one object or one piece of furniture *"en souvenir.* I only buy things I love for my house," he says, "just as I do for my shop. In any purchase, I just follow my heart."

White walls highlight the deep-green trim of the wide wood stairway that winds from the stone-tiled foyer up to the second floor. The Greek key design of the fabric on the upholstered chair, the urn on a pedestal, and the carved pediment of the balustrade are charming classical elements that give the hall an old-fashioned air.

An umbrella stand in the foyer bursts with parasols and canes, collected and inherited by Monsieur Gosselin.

ART OF THE MENUISIER

As in every other aspect of French life of the 17th and 18th centuries, the craft of furniture making had its own hierarchies through the guild system. The *ébéniste,* whose cabinetmaking included the delicate art of veneering, was at the top of his trade. For lesser items, such as carved plain wood chairs and tables, clients sought out the *menuisier* (joiner). Other contributing trades were the *sculpteur,* who produced the carving; the *fondeur-ciseleur,* who fashioned

An elaborate petit point tapestry whose pattern softly harmonizes with those of the curtain, screen, and rug covers a Louis XV fauteuil from the Ile-de-France, right. *A coiffeuse d'homme (man's dressing table),* below, *is a simple but elegant representation of the transition between the styles of Louis XV and Louis XVI. The lamp was created from a 19th-century architectural element with its original paint.*

metal mounts; the *doreur,* who gilded both wood and mounts; and the *tapissier,* who upholstered the results.

For most homes, the *menuisier*'s fine craft sufficed to create the few pieces essential for everyday living. In time, as the guilds were abolished after the Revolution and the tastes of Parisians changed, distinctions between types of furniture makers blurred. The village woodworkers and itinerant artisans who traveled from property to property followed royal trends, but their products were more basic, rustic, and unadorned. In the small towns outside of Paris, well-to-do families might own a range of pieces, rather than a suite of furniture produced in a particular style. Less grand than the products of the state ateliers, these simple chests and chairs were nonetheless as elegant as they were practical.

A sturdy 18th-century buffet from the Ile-de-France, right, *holds a rare collection of blue-on-white Chantilly and Sèvres porcelain.*

Seventeenth-century coffee mills, like the boxwood and iron one, top, *are rarely found intact. Blown and engraved by hand, the 18th-century glassware,* above, *was seen on country tables throughout the Ile-de-France.*

A carved Louis XIV commode supports an expressive stone sculpture of the Flight of the Holy Family, a small clock, and a lamp fashioned from a Chinese vase, below.

Two sculpted amours *(cupids) poised on a marble pedestal greet visitors,* above, *in the Château de Champs. The handsome proportions and delicate lines of the 18th-century* secrétaire, *left,* indicate that it was made in the Ile-de-France.*

AN ANCIENT PRIORY

The 17th-century priory of Les Dames de Saint-Rémy, an adjoining 18th-century stone house, and the remains of the 13th-century Chapel of Sainte-Bathilde are today the residence of a charming former Parisienne who has all but abandoned the city in favor of the historic town of Senlis. The ancient royal heart of the Ile-de-France, where Hugues Capet was crowned as the first king of France in 987, Senlis is a handsome stone town with a 12th-century cathedral, a feudal château royal, a web of narrow old streets, and the remains of a Gallo-Roman arena. Here, impressed by the rich history and enchanted by the house friends of hers had just offered for sale, the current *propriétaire* decided to make a new life.

The long two-story facade of this Senlis home flanks a narrow cobbled road in the heart of town. The entrance leads into a black-and-white stone-tiled foyer that opens directly onto a spacious garden shaded by old apple trees and a 150-year-old walnut tree. Nearby are the remains of the Sainte-Bathilde chapel, now reworked into a garage. The rooms of the house, illuminated by tall mullioned windows, are furnished in 17th- and 18th-century family furniture, dominated by the styles of Louis XV and XVI, but intermingled here and there with Napoleon III and contemporary sofas. Le Manach, Braquenié, and Hamot fabrics enhance the elegant *vieille France* atmosphere.

Old-fashioned and at the same time what the French call *branché* (literally, "plugged in" or "up-to-the-minute"), the décor is also quintessentially French. Originally, however, the owner had something quite different in

An imposing 18th-century stone house adjoining a 17th-century priory in Senlis, above and right, *is protected by ancient stone walls covered with climbing flowers and vines. Directly in front of the arched entrance rises a 150-year-old walnut tree.*

mind. "When I first started decorating the house," she recalls, "I wanted a house that was completely English—I loved the look of English country furnishings and fabrics. But nothing worked, nothing seemed comfortable in its place. The house, I realized, simply refused this English invasion, in spite of all my efforts. Everything English had to go, replaced with French fabrics and furniture. Both the house and I are now very comfortable."

Originally decorated by the current owner in an English country style which she says the house "refused," all the rooms are now imbued with a pure vieille France *atmosphere. In the white-beamed living room,* above, *walls and overstuffed sofas are covered in fabric by Le Manach. Atop a piano is an antique* boîte à perruques *(wig box). Adorning the walls of the living room,* left, *are old family portraits, some displayed in majestic gilt frames. Louis XIII walnut end tables covered with antique tapestries flank the sofa by the window. In the foreground is a sumptuous Napoleon III armchair. The velvet-upholstered sofas behind it date from the same period. In the window beneath the scalloped sheers is a delicately worked Victorian-epoch birdcage,* right.

A small, beguiling young girl's bedroom, with rose walls and white trim, above, is furnished with a painted Louis XVI bed.

In the corner of a small guest bedroom, above, a fruitwood étagère displays an antique clock and round boxes in woven-straw marquetry. The fabric covering the walls is from Le Manach. The fabric surrounding the black marble Louis Philippe mantel in another bedroom, right, is a toile de Jouy in the pattern called Dame Blanche.

Fabric in a potted flower print from Braquenié covers the walls of a second-floor bedroom, left, furnished with an Ile-de-France Louis XVI bed in natural wood and a marble-topped mahogany commode from the same period. A Napoleon III bathtub commands center stage, above, in the master bathroom. Terra-cotta tiles cover the floor. Set by the window, the low painted chair with rush seat is called a chaise de foyer.

An 18th-century wrought-iron grille with a full skirt of yellow and magenta flowers at its base borders the far end of the garden, above and right. *Ancient stone steps,* far right, *lead up beyond the wall at the back of the garden.*

Old apple trees, above, *in front of the ivy-covered remains of an ancient chapel, shade and scent the spacious garden. Sprigs from the sprawling apple tree creep through the wrought-iron grille,* right. *Pink creepers, planted years ago, have firmly established themselves against the old stones of the garden wall,* far right.

PART FOUR
Rustique et Rural
DEEP COUNTRY

Several families of Suffolk sheep, left, *gather under the flowering apple trees at the Bergerie Nationale in Rambouillet. A young gendarme,* above, *pedals to his post along a tranquil country lane.*

FOR THOSE WHO SEEK THE GOOD LIFE IN FIELD AND FOREST, THE BEST OF THE ILE-DE-FRANCE IS ITS COUNTRYSIDE, WHERE THE REFINED SPIRIT MINGLES WITH THE PLEASURES OF SIMPLE LIVING.

The residences tucked into the beautiful exurban countryside, more than any other aspect of the province, exemplify the *esprit raffiné* of the true Ile-de-France. Stylish, tasteful, and at the same time profoundly pastoral, the deep-country homes of the Ile-de-France have enticed Parisians out of the capital for 200 years. For summer sojourns or weekend escapes, this is the landscape of an urbanite's dreams.

The fantasy encompasses the ultimate classic of well-to-do recreation: the Ile-de-France is horse country, with stag hunts, stud farms, and woodland *randonnées* (excursions) on horseback. The landscape for these open-air adventures is spotted here and there, on a hillside or through the trees, with majestic medieval abbeys basking in their physical and spiritual isolation, and sumptuous 17th- and 18th-century châteaux spreading over still-vast seigneurial domains. Old mills

and weathered farmhouses, most converted now into comfortable or even luxurious dwellings, are the real estate of choice for living in these splendid environs. Touching on the outermost corners of the region and penetrating the deepest forest glens, here is the essential, and the ideal, Ile-de-France.

In a classic Ile-de-France landscape, left, *the houses and church of a small village over-look striated fields of wheat, while a gentle rise of woodland forms a verdant backdrop. Azaleas,* above left, *bloom in many domestic gardens in the province. The thatched-roof buildings of Marie Antoinette's Hameau,* above, *on the grounds of Versailles, represent a queen's vision of rustic bliss. In the heart of horse country, a 19th-century hobbyhorse from Chantilly's Musée Vivant du Cheval (Living Museum of the Horse) briefly sees the light of day,* right.

AN AGELESS MILL HOUSE

If it were not for the screams of peacocks shattering the tranquility of the Moulin de Chiennat from time to time, a visitor to this ancient mill house draped in willows might become lost completely in the unreal beauty of the setting. Invisible from the rural road that runs along the wheat fields of the 12-acre property, the Moulin de Chiennat sits surrounded by water on three sides deep in the open countryside near Provins, 55 miles southeast of Paris. A veritable arboretum of oak, poplar, walnut, cherry, plum, cedar, as well as willow shades the grounds and obscures the house from view. The name Chiennat is derived from the Old French word for *chêne* (oak tree). Also gracing the property is an exotic array of birds and animals: keeping company with the vociferous peacocks are Japanese hens, Chinese roosters, ducks, geese, pigeons, dogs, and donkeys.

A vision of serenity, the Moulin de Chiennat, a mill house built in the 14th century and restored in the 18th, left, *seen from the rear and,* top, *the ivy-covered front facade, is sheltered from the road by a veil of poplars, willows, oaks, and cedars. Residing in the screened-in cages on the back lawn is a lively community of Japanese hens, Chinese roosters, and peacocks. Nearby, ducks glide on the pond,* above.

The mill dates from the 14th century, when it ground wheat for a nearby feudal lord and his serfs. In the mid-1700s the Abbot Terray, who built the nearby Château de la Motte-Tilly (see pages 29 to 45), bought the mill, restoring and expanding it to 18th-century standards. Over the next 200 years the property belonged to a duke, a miller, a traveling piano salesman, a young local couple who came to grief when the husband drowned trying to unblock the old millwheel, and an old woman who was a member of the Resistance in World War II. In 1971 the house was purchased by two Parisians who had been seeking a country home on the water. They had written to all the real estate agents in the region, and finally one proposed the property, which had been on the market for five years. "We managed to buy the place for fifty percent less than an offer that had been refused five years earlier," says one of the owners.

The Moulin de Chiennat is a hard place to leave. Although it was bought originally as a vacation house, the owners found they spent more and more of their time in their idyllic hideaway. Today they reside at the mill house full time, making occasional trips to Paris for business or culture. Friends and neighbors seem to be constantly in attendance, dropping by for an aperitif, dinner, or the weekend. From autumn to early spring a large leg of lamb or rib of beef frequently roasts *à la ficelle* (by a string) over a crackling wood fire in the kitchen's wide stone hearth. The capacious house and grounds accommodate a score of visitors without ever giving the sense of a crowd.

Books fill the walls to the rafters and over the windows in the second-floor library, above. *An amusing trompe l'oeil book design painted on the inside of the shutters adds interest to the room at night. A handsome 18th-century stone fireplace dominates a second-floor salon,* right. *A 19th-century rustic banquette with floral cushions provides seating by the front window, while two overstuffed paisley cushions on the opposite side of the fireplace offer additional seating.*

The mill's interior, renovated slowly over the years, is decorated with a range of antiques from the homely to the grand. One of the owners, a collector and a dealer, created the decorative mélange with a discerning eye and a profound confidence in his taste. Here, every detail is perfectly realized. This owner buys and sells antiques for a living at les Puces, the Paris flea market, and the antiques that ultimately find no buyers come home to the Moulin de Chiennat. "I love the unsalable," he says. The house is full of intriguing *objets* with a very personal appeal.

"I don't specialize in any particular country or period. What I look for is character and a special rapport between form and material; a piece could be French or English, rustic or sophisticated, 17th, 18th, or 19th century. Not everything here is of great value, but each piece in its own way is unique." Bearing witness to this eclectic approach to collecting are 19th-

An antique glass-paned door of carved oak opens onto one of the second-floor bedrooms, most of which are warmed by their own fireplaces.

century apothecary jars holding olive oil, a rustic Louis XV farm table, 17th-century stone tiles from Burgundy, a hand-painted English Regency screen, and the polychrome figurehead from an 18th-century French man-o'-war.

Remarkably, considering the eclectic range of collector's items, the house is supremely livable; one feels comfortable everywhere. The strains of a Rossini opera float out of the open window. The only element that detracts from the perfection of this scene are the persistent mosquitoes. "Every rose has its thorns," says one of the owners with a smile. "The Moulin de Chiennat has mosquitoes."

In stark contrast to the rough-timbered walls of a bedroom, a gilt-framed portrait of a 19th-century aristocrat tops a small, charming 18th-century commode created in the Ile-de-France.

227

Under the rough-hewn beams of a small bedroom, two guests can sleep in cozy intimacy in a rustic 19th-century lit clos *(box bed),* left. *An intriguing variety of light fixtures illuminates rooms throughout the house:* above, *a delicately wrought 18th-century candelabrum sconce;* right, *a table lamp created from a 19th-century candlestick shines on an antique decoy in an Empire-style bedroom.*

A small, distinctive guest bathroom with a masculine air contains an Empire-epoch bathtub; the late 19th-century porcelain sink stands on a classical pedestal. In an unusual touch for a bathroom, black brocade curtains drape the window.

A small, arched stained-glass window evokes the impression of a shrine in the master bathroom, with the dramatic copper-and-zinc Empire bathtub as the altar. An Oriental carpet partially covers the terra-cotta floor for the benefit of bathers exiting from the tub. The 19th-century mahogany shaving stand is English.

A simple and sparsely furnished guest room under the eaves is en-hanced by a gracefully sculpted Louis XV fireplace and mantel. A turn-of-the-century wire birdcage awaits an occupant.

The rustic "summer room" off the dining room and opening onto the front terrace once held the mill-wheel mechanism. Today the room is occasionally used for casual dinners in warm weather, but functions primarily as a storage area. In the suspended screen cage against the wall, assorted cheeses remain temperate, ripening slowly. Below the cheeses, a long farm table holds homemade jams, pickles, and vinegar.

Large, dramatic country garden bouquets displayed in antique pitchers, urns, gueridons, and vases brighten almost every room of the Moulin de Chiennat. In a vision à la Van Gogh, huge sunflowers in an antique salt-glazed pitcher glow like miniature suns on a small tile-bordered stone sink in the kitchen.

In the pink-walled dining room, left, *an arrangement of lacy wild-flowers placed on an 18th-century marble-topped hunt table soars almost to the ceiling beams. By the kitchen door, an enormous floral bouquet gathered from the property is massed in a terra-cotta pot,* above.

In the dining room, right, *as in other rooms of the house, the rough and rustic interior elements are in marked contrast to the sophistication and refinement of the furnishings—setting both off to advantage. Under the teal-blue beams, a 19th-century English mahogany table with accompanying leather-seated armchairs accommodates eight for dinner. The 19th-century oak cabinet against the far wall,* above, *holds a 19th-century English dinner service of blue-and-white* pâte-tendre *(soft-paste porcelain).*

A deep green enamel-and-brass stove from the 1920s enlivens a corner of the kitchen next to the large rustic hearth that is also used for cooking. Stacked between them is a collection of antique English copperware.

The deep green of the stove appears again as trim for a shelf that runs across the wall above the old stone sink with a blue-and-white tiled backsplash.

A kitchen drawer opens to reveal several sets of French and English 19th-century silverware in casual array.

A long 19th-century harvest table can welcome a crowd in the kitchen. Seating on one side is provided by a simple bench, while on the other side an austere 19th-century church pew cheered by striped cushions seats a half-dozen diners. The kitchen's unusual lobster bisque shade is a custom mixture of old-fashioned powdered pigments, purchased at a store going out of business and mixed with water and alcohol. The color changes with the humidity, becoming more intense when the air is moist, softer and paler when the air is dry.

241

An outdoor table on the front terrace, *left, is laid for a casual summer lunch with friends.* Below left, *as sunset approaches, a gaggle of geese gathers at a round lawn table scavenging for crumbs. Windows on the rear facade, in the right-hand section of the structure that once held the mill housing, were installed for function rather than symmetry. Peacocks, such as the fellow with the dazzling plumage,* below, *strut freely over the property.*

The Moulin de Chiennat's three resident canines wait expectantly at the property's tall wrought-iron gates for their masters' return. Behind the gates, vast wheatfields stretch out to a small country road.

MARIE ANTOINETTE'S HAMEAU

Even Marie Antoinette, one of the most lavish queens in history, had a simple side. Longing to escape —briefly—the extravagant trappings of Louis XVI's court, the queen wished to live the bucolic life with a little house, a vegetable garden, and a stable of animals. To indulge his beloved mate (said at the time to be growing discontented with her husband), Louis XVI built for her Le Hameau—the Hamlet—on the grounds of Versailles' extensive park. Le Hameau was designed as a tiny, rustic Norman village, with 10 half-timbered maisonettes topped by thatched or flat-tiled roofs, a small dairy, a fishing hut, a dovecote, and the larger *Maison de la Reine* (Queen's House).

Built near the Petit Trianon, Le Hameau was a fantasy of the simple life that the queen craved. The architect Richard Mique and the painter Hubert Robert collaborated to design a lake and a little village around the bank. Here, in a Gallic variation of fiddling while Rome burned, Marie Antoinette harvested her tender vegetables while the seeds of revolt took root in Paris.

A cluster of small buildings designed to resemble a rustic hamlet on the grounds of Versailles, Le Hameau is an 18th-century pastoral fantasy. The Maison de la Reine (Queen's House), above left and left, *has covered galleries reached by a spiral wood staircase. The Mill House,* right, *thickly covered with vines, still has a working water wheel.*

A RUSTIC RETREAT

When Monsieur Philippe and his wife, Abigail, first saw their 18th-century farmhouse, it was shortly after dusk. The sun had set and the property was enveloped in darkness. "We walked in and immediately felt *chez nous*—at home," recalls Philippe. The house, in the northwest corner of the Ile-de-France, almost at the border of Normandy, was built of limestone quarried in the region and roofed with terra-cotta tiles. The property's three acres, the house, and the outbuildings— barn, stable, and 17th-century gatekeeper's cottage—accommodate the busy and diverse family life of Philippe and Abigail. With four children between them—his two and her two from former marriages—who come and go as they please, the house is often in a lively state of flux.

Set in a tiny village almost at the border of Normandy, this 18th-century farmhouse was constructed in locally quarried limestone. The 17th-century gatekeeper's cottage, above left, now houses the family's household help. A thick blanket of ivy obscures the front of the house, left.

Both antiques enthusiasts, Philippe and Abigail use their stone barn as a workshop, restoring country-style furniture in its cool, airy rooms. Horseback riding is another shared passion; the stable holds their two horses, Peer Gynt and Jolie. Some mornings Philippe and Abigail enjoy a canter through the neighboring fields and woodland before heading off to work in Paris.

"The Ile-de-France is a very peaceful part of France," says Philippe, "particularly our area. It's really 'la France Profonde' [Deep France]. You can't feel Paris from here, and yet it's only half an hour

away. For being so close to the city, our town is amazingly provincial. Some of my neighbors have never been to Paris!"

After purchasing their retreat in the early 1980s, Philippe and Abigail set about restoring the interior. Once somber even at high noon, the rooms brightened under several coats of white paint. In the kitchen, white-glazed tiles

gave the room vibrancy and glow Major changes included redefining the functions of several rooms: what is now a small study was once the house's only bathroom; the entryway with its stone floor and big Dutch oven used to be the kitchen; and the well-used living room used to be *la réception*—the formal parlor used only for special occasions. Some elements of the house remained intact. "We found some of the ceiling beams painted an intriguing shade of blue and we left them that way," Philippe says. They also found the property almost overgrown with old rose-bushes, which they tamed by vigorous weeding and pruning. The roses attract large, lazy bees, whose persistent buzzing is the loudest noise to be heard in this rustic country domain on a lazy summer afternoon.

Philippe and Abigail, left, *take a moment's respite from rearranging country-style antiques in the stone-walled barn, now used for furniture restoration. Daughter Gaudérique,* above, *grooms Jolie, one of the family's two horses, in the stable, as Peer Gynt watches from his stall.*

A shallow stone sink in the entrée of the house, *left, testifies to the fact that the room's original function was as a kitchen. The blue beams partially visible above the doorway and,* right, *in another view of the* entrée, *were painted in that shade by the previous owners. Philippe and Abigail painted the wall by the door a softer blue to harmonize. The armoire is an early-18th-century piece made in Brittany.*

A basketful of cut roses from the garden, left, *fills the* entrée *with a heady sweet perfume as they wilt in the warmth of a summer day.*

Directly across from the Breton armoire in the entrée *is the original fireplace,* above, *inset with a Dutch oven, once used for cooking family meals and baking bread. The sensuous sculptural lines of a French mid-19th-century wrought-iron rocking chair draws the eye to a corner of the book-lined living room,* right.

The second-floor hallway, with well-polished 18th-century terra-cotta floor, *left, leads past the sculpted door of a guest room on the way to the master bedroom. A painted 19th-century armoire for towels and a large bathtub tiled in a mosaic of variegated blues are the main features of the master bath,* below.

In the master bedroom, left, *a Louis XV chair partners an 18th-century occasional table supporting a wood statue of a dandy, ca. 1850. A 19th-century provincial chest,* below, *displays a collection of 19th-century wood flacons used to hold various toiletries.*

A large rug cushions the impact on the airy kitchen's slate-tiled floor. One long harvest table serves as a worktable while another is for dining. The 19th-century pine buffet à deux-corps (here used for table- and glassware) is from the Ile-de-France, but shows the strong influence of Normandy, the neighboring province to the west.

A series of small paned windows overlooking the back garden illuminates the kitchen at noon, as preparations get underway for a picnic.

Tables are set under the old willows in the backyard for a déjeuner sur l'herbe, *left. On the simple but satisfying menu are melon, Parma ham, baked ham, salami in crushed-pepper crust, peasant bread, a garden salad of lettuce and chives, a cheese platter, an apricot tart, and red and white wine—a Beaujolais and a Sancerre. Philippe and Abigail,* right, *exercise Jolie and Peer Gynt at the far end of the property. Beyond a bank of old rosebushes lining a garden path,* below right, *three old deck chairs are arranged for an after-lunch nap in the sun.*

THE HUNT

Hunting for stag, buck, or wild boar has been an aristocratic pastime for hundreds of years in France. *Pavillons de chasse* or *relais de chasse* (hunting lodges) dating from the 15th century still dot the countryside in many regions. The art of the chase probably reached its zenith in the 18th century, under the influence of Louis XV and his grandson, Louis XVI, when most of today's rituals of the hunt were refined from rules dating from the reign of François I in the early 1500s. Aristocrats in pre-Revolutionary France hunted every day in every season, accompanied by their packs of hounds, their pointsmen, their whippers-in, and their kennelmen.

Contemporary aficionados of the hunt, such as the group of classically attired hunters photographed here during a late fall hunt deep in the forest of Chantilly, follow an immutable drill. Explained by Yves Bienaimé, a member of the Chantilly hunt and founder and director of Chantilly's Musée Vivant du Cheval, a traditional hunt begins with the hunters gathered in a semicircle to hear the report of the pointsmen who have reconnoitered the prey, usually a stag, at dawn,

Released just before the stag hunt begins, a pack of hounds, below, *explores the forest turf. Hunters and hounds,* right, *make their way along an* allée *deep in the forest of Chantilly on the morning of an early winter hunt.*

memorizing its tracks and discovering its covert. The master of the hunt, the day's interlocutor, decides how to deploy the hunters, and they then set off on horseback armed only with brass horns. The packs of hounds yapping at the horses' heels, tails wagging stiffly with excitement, have been expertly trained to respond to horn or voice. The hunt ends when the prey is tired, trapped, and ultimately brought down by the hounds. The slaughtered animal's right forefoot is ceremoniously offered by the leading whipper-in to the master of the hunt, after which the horns sound the farewell.

Yves Bienaimé, the rider second from the left and founder-director of Chantilly's Musée Vivant du Cheval, heads down a forest path with three fellow huntsmen, all dressed in their hunt club's traditional habit bleu *(blue riding habit) and armed only with brass horns.*

The master of hounds, left, readies his pack with a few forceful words and a strong grip as the hunt is about to start. Before the action begins, the dogs are allowed to run free, below right, but they never stray far from the center of activity. Right, local observers of the hunt gather, casquettes on their heads, binoculars in hand, to follow the action through the woods, passing judgment all the way. The day's master of the hunt, center right, on this day one of the few women members of the club, interrogates the pointsmen, far right, on the whereabouts and behavior of the stag.

AN ANTIQUAIRE'S ECLECTIC ENCLAVE

The rural road through the wheat fields of Mondreville runs by the unprepossessing stone walls of Pierre and Isabelle Chalvignac's country compound. The only hint that this home is different from its modest provincial neighbors is the small sign, ANTIQUITES, directing passersby into the driveway. Just inside its small enclosed *place* this late 18th-century farm bears the touch of a master restorer and *collectionneur*. Renaissance columns sculpted of stone, carved 17th-century doors, unusual hand-hewn stones and an 18th-century marble goddess enhance the simple grace and neat proportions of the property.

Antiques dealers Pierre and Isabelle Chalvignac, above, *restored their late-18th-century farmhouse, adding antique architectural "found objects." The farm's former* grange, left, *now houses the antiques shop.*

The Chalvignacs' antiques shop is installed in the former *grange,* or barn. Paris collectors and dealers alike know the Chalvignacs' enterprise as a source of high-quality 17th- and 18th-century antique furniture and *objets* at extremely fair prices. The Chalvignacs live across the courtyard. A wing extending from the house to the *grange* walls unites the two structures. "When we bought the place in 1968," Pierre relates, "it was a dilapidated farm. Bit by bit we've restored it. Every time I found an old stone or an old door I put it in." The Chalvignacs made an effort not to have too uniform or "finished" a look. "We didn't want symmetry—two doors here, two doors there; a column here, a column there," says Pierre. "We also tried not to clean the old elements too much, to avoid a newly restored look."

The interior of the Chalvignacs' home bears even less resemblance to its former life as a farmer's dwelling than the exterior. Sophisticated faux marbre and trompe l'oeil detailing painted on walls, tables, and doors give, as Pierre remarks, "an *esprit dix-huitième*" to the rooms. An

Extending from the grange *to the main house, a long, low wing has a treillaged facade and a timbered covered doorway leading to an office and guest rooms,* left. *In humorous juxtaposition, a noble 19th-century bust,* above right, *sits on a pedestal before the peeling walls that separate two of the* grange's *former stall doors. A stone stairway, originally built to reach the former hayloft in the* grange, right, *now leads to a second-floor workroom.*

eclectic assemblage of antique elements—18th-century terra-cotta tiles, carved paneling, and even elegant door pulls—gives the rooms additional character. While the Chalvignacs' house today is a harmonious blend of 18th-century style with 20th-century talent and taste, the look evolved over a long period of time. The Chalvignac style is very personal, almost organic, without the stamp of an urban decorator. As a decorating philosophy, they favor attention to detail. "Even three stones," Pierre notes, "can change a room."

An esprit dix-huitième—*18th-century spirit—pervades the Chalvignacs' living room,* right, *dominated by shades of saffron, terra-cotta, and antique green. The fireplace, the pedestal to the right of the fireplace, and the low square table in the center of the room (detail, left) are modern interpretations of 18th-century faux marbre. Above the fireplace a covered wood medallion,* above, *is one of an original group of four representing the elements in a pot-au-feu—fish, fruits, vegetables, and meat.*

The dining room door with its intricate handle and latch was once part of the boiserie of a grand château. Pierre Chalvignac painted it in trompe l'oeil to match the rest of the room, and changed its glass panes for four antique mirrors.

A variety of antique objets grace the Chalvignacs' dining room, left. The sophisticated trompe l'oeil boiserie stands out against the original exposed beams, painted white. The 18th-century octagonal terra-cotta floor tiles from a provincial château were created to be laid flush, but here are laid with diagonal spacers between them because, as Pierre Chalvignac explains, "there weren't enough of them to lay the conventional way, so we improvised." One of the room's most beguiling objects is a painted 18th-century clay statuette of a little girl, right, inspired by the pastoral, romantic paintings of François Boucher and created for a greenhouse.

271

NONPAREIL SHEEP FARM AND DAIRY

There are sheep farms and then there is the Bergerie Nationale of Rambouillet. Constructed in 1786 by Louis XVI on the grounds of the Château de Rambouillet, the Bergerie (Sheep Farm) was dedicated to developing rare breeds of sheep as well as exploring other aspects of animal husbandry. Louis XVI had France's first merino sheep brought to this early experimental farm from Spain, which had a virtual monopoly at the time on the production of fine wool. The Bergerie today, part of the Zoo-technological Training Center of Rambouillet, continues its studies into sheep raising; here early studies in artificial insemination were conducted after World War II. Meanwhile, oblivious to their elite stature, merinos and a strain of Suffolk sheep graze and gambol under the gnarled old apple trees in the surrounding orchards.

Created three years before the Revolution, the Bergerie Nationale maintains its classical lines, above right, *and its primary functions of sheep husbandry more than 200 years later. Steps lead to a large, restored dovecote,* left, *topped by a bronze cupola,* right. *Suffolk sheep,* below, *graze on the Bergerie's rich pastureland.*

Half a mile away from the historic Bergerie is the Laiterie (Dairy) de la Reine, built for a bored Marie Antoinette, who accompanied the king on his hunting sojourns to Rambouillet. A royal hunting ground since the 14th century, Rambouillet's château and park were acquired by Louis from the duc de Penthièvre. The pristine Laiterie, which resembles nothing so much as a mausoleum, was built of sandstone deep within the park that stretched out from the château. It is divided into two large rotundas: the first, entered through large double doors, is dominated by an enormous round marble table, where the churning, skimming, and sealing in containers were supposed to take place; opening onto this workroom is a vaulted room with a sculpted ceiling and a massive, man-made rock formation creating a large grotto. A fountain supplying fresh water is adorned with a marble statue by Pierre Julien of a nymph guiding the goat Amalthée, which, according to legend, nursed the baby Jupiter. The statue, which won the sculptor the Prix de Rome, is called *La Chevrière* (The Goat Girl). Here, in the refreshing tranquility and coolness of the grotto, Marie Antoinette came to escape the confines of the château, which she liked to call *la crapaudière* (loosely translated, "the stinkhole"). Luminescent and elegantly proportioned, the Laiterie, like a lavish stage set, has beauty but no soul, empty now of any signs of previous human activity. In the queen's dairy, neither a bucket nor a ladle remains.

Built at about the same time as the Bergerie Nationale, the Laiterie de la Reine is a showpiece of elegant classical style, resembling, from the outside, right, *a mausoleum. Fancy pediments surmount the doors,* top left, *which open into a luminous marble-floored rotunda with a round marble worktable,* left. *The first rotunda opens onto a second, larger one,* far right, *also marble floored, and dominated by a large grotto with a fresh-water fountain.*

A COUNTRY IDYLL

Finding Birgitta and Olivier Fouret's country place for the first time can be a challenge. Set discreetly behind a tiny farm hamlet, it is nevertheless just minutes off the Chartres-Orléans autoroute, and easy to reach once the rural byways become familiar. Scarcely more than one-half hour south of Paris, the Fourets' domain was once the mill house and barracks of the Maréchal de Plessis-Mornay. Four acres, including a river and pond, surround an enclave of 17th-century stone buildings: the original mill house, the Fourets' residence; the former *colombier* (dovecote), now the children's

Lovingly restored by Birgitta and Olivier Fouret (above, with *daughters Natascha, at far right, and Katarina) the Moulin des Echelettes, a 17th-century mill house set on a lushly landscaped property, is a beguiling weekend and holiday retreat from Paris. Les Echelettes,* right, *enjoys views on three sides of the placidly flowing La Remarde River.*

cottage; and the old barn, with an apartment for the caretakers.

Tall ranks of willows, poplars, and linden trees line the banks of the narrow river, La Remarde, that flows, perpetually gurgling, through the property. Nature has richly embellished the Moulin des Echelettes, the centuries-old name of the Fourets' home, with both flora and fauna. In the distance beyond the children's cottage, cows, sheep, and ponies graze under the linden trees, a 19th-century English landscape come to life. Banks of ivy nearly hide the stone facades of the main house and the cottage, while wisteria garlands the first-floor windows. In the midst of this natural glory, a plump goldfish swims around and around in a stone-walled pond.

The Fourets' neighbors are horse breeders, as are several other nearby residents. In this part of the province, horse lovers predominate. A popular weekend pastime for the locals is a vigorous point-to-point, or steeplechase, competition. Olivier, once a polo player on the international circuit, still rides almost every day he is at home, while Birgitta gardens or cooks.

An intriguing collection of antique French and English canes and walking sticks catches the eye just inside the main house entrance, paved in 18th-century terra-cotta tiles, as is the kitchen, seen through the door.

The sofa, armchairs, and an ottoman in the beamed living room, top, are covered in fabric from the Paris house of Braquenié. The mid-19th-century hand-painted screen with a floral motif in the corner is English. Adjoining the living room is the library, above. Set before Olivier's rolltop Louis XVI desk is a 19th-century Swedish armchair. In a corner of the living room, right, an antique Louis XVI tric-trac game table holds an array of Birgitta's collectibles, among them a statue of Aristotle, a collection of ivory billiard balls, a mid-19th-century French landscape painting, and a tall 19th-century mahogany obelisk.

Clustered collections and souvenirs add warmth and distinct personality throughout the house. Niched in a hallway alcove are snapshots from Olivier's days playing competitive polo, left. Two 19th-century blackamoor figures stand before the lamp. In an upstairs guest bedroom, above, Birgitta's collection of 19th-century watercolor portraits of English houses adorns the walls. Family photographs and mementos are atop a cachemire-covered table in the master bedroom, top.

The Fourets are a peripatetic couple. Olivier, an international business consultant, travels frequently. Birgitta is the proprietor of Haga, a small, intriguing antiques shop at 22 rue de Grenelle in Paris, full of bibelots, some furniture, and her specialty—antique *cachemire* shawls, intricately handwoven paisleys from old India. Birgitta travels to antiques fairs throughout France, and often flies to London for special sales. Her career as an *antiquaire* developed from a passion for beautiful old things and a talent for decorating that blossomed when she was one of the world's top models in the 1960s. A native of Sweden, Birgitta, then Birgitta von Klecker, was discovered by Diana Vreeland while vacationing one summer in Dark Harbor, Maine, and her elegantly sculpted features and dark blond hair soon graced the covers of *Vogue* and *Harper's Bazaar.* In the 1970s, living in New York, she turned her creative talents to decorating her country house in Water Mill, Long Island. Her efforts quickly came to the attention of several design magazines, which featured her work and launched her on a second career as decorator. In 1980 she married Olivier, and the two settled in Paris. With their daughter, Kata-

The remains of Sunday breakfast—a brioche ring—awaits nibbles on the kitchen counter's blue-and-white Dèvres tiles, above. *The handsome and sophisticated country kitchen,* right, *belies its former function— housing the enormous mill wheel that once turned as water flowed through the base of the room. The heavily beamed kitchen is trimmed in black to match Birgitta's collection of 19th-century Japanese teapots on the mantel.*

rina, and Birgitta's two teenage children from an earlier marriage, Sébastien and Natascha, the Fourets make a lively household.

In the early years of their marriage, Olivier and Birgitta had a country house not far from their present property in Dourdan. Occasionally they would pass by the Moulin des Echelettes and sigh, so closely did it resemble their dream house. When it finally came up for sale, the Fourets snapped it up almost before the A VENDRE sign was staked into the ground.

The older children's quarters in the former dovecote have a kitchen and a large, luminous white-and-blue bathroom, tiled by Birgitta over 10 recent August days. Katarına sleeps in a small, charming bedroom decorated in bright Provençal fabrics down the hall from her parents' bedroom in the main house. Beautiful fabrics

Birgitta purchased provincial cotton fabric from the Marché Saint-Pierre in Paris, and had it made into quilts, floor poufs, and a dressing table skirt for the guest bedroom.

and a collection of Birgitta's trademark *cachemires* distinguish many of the rooms, as do handsome pieces of furniture, some heirlooms, others recent finds. The pieces range from Olivier's Louis XVI rolltop desk in the library to the whimsical 19th-century English *chameau,* or camel, a leather-and-wood beast of burden designed to hold tossed-on coats, capes, and wraps in the *entrée.* The house, within and without, is a photographer's dream. With her keen eye and sure sense of style, Birgitta has created a home photogenic from every angle.

Tile lines the tub area in the bathroom of the children's cottage, above right. *In Katarina's small bedroom down the hall from her parents', a cheerful Souleiado print cotton fabric has been used in making the bedcovers and bolsters of the 19th-century bed, upholstering the chair, and creating the minicanopy draped from the wall over the head- and footboards,* right.

Old stone walls massed with flow-ers not only hide Les Echelettes from the road, but also separate one terraced level from another, far left and left. *Simple wood gar-den furniture by Tectona,* below left, *accommodates the family for an alfresco lunch or dinner under the apple trees. Katarina, with horses* below, *makes the most of the country life.*

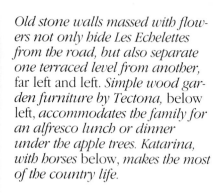

Wisteria climbs the old stone walls around the doorway that leads into the main house's foyer, left. A mossy duo of bears left over from Christmas sits in the window of the children's cottage, above.

Restaurant
Les
Préjugés
Henri Scoffier
Tél. 34-86-22-65

PORTFOLIO

IN THE ILE-DE-FRANCE

*T*he Ile-de-France permits even the short-term visitor to Paris to experience the pleasures and charm of the rural French countryside in just an afternoon. For residents of the capital, as well as visitors endowed with more leisure, the Ile-de-France provides an easily accessible rustic haven for weekends and holidays away from the city. The attractions of this gracious region are plentiful. The entire province is rich in quality antiques shops, small museums, and châteaux, as well as lavish parks open to the public. Fairs and festivals fill the provincial calendar, providing themes and destinations, were they needed, for outings into the hinterlands throughout the year. Here, in our personal portfolio, are sources and suggestions for shopping, sightseeing, and staying in the Ile-de-France. *Bon voyage dans l'Ile-de-France!*

ANTIQUES

The Ile-de-France is a rich source for those in quest of high-quality antique furniture and *objets.* Furniture production by skilled artisans was prolific in the 17th, 18th, and 19th centuries, and much of the furniture, implements, and bibelots produced in earlier centuries remains, or has returned. A broad range of antique merchandise can be found in the Ile-de-France, with some items

and styles particularly well represented: handsome rustic 18th- and 19th-century furniture in oak and wild cherry; Louis XV, XVI, Directoire, and especially Louis Philippe commodes, desks, secretaries, armoires, buffet cabinets, night tables, and rush-seated chairs. Antique kitchenware—copperware, cauldrons, kettles, casseroles, and silverware—is also widely available. Dealers in the Val d'Oise *département,* in northwestern Ile-de-France near the Normandy border, often carry antique pine furniture with strong Norman influence, as well as 19th-century faience from Creil. An asterisk in the listing denotes the major *antiquaires* in town.

As we have noted in our previous books, the best and most comprehensive guide for serious antiquing in France is the *Guide Emer,* an annual publication listing dealers by region and specialty and available in bookstores and some kiosks throughout France. It can also be ordered directly from: Guide Emer, 50 rue Quai de l'Hôtel de Ville, 75004 Paris, France. *ABC Décor, Trouvailles,* and *Estampilles* are three other useful publications, with features on antiques and collectibles and up-to-the-minute listings of fairs and shows throughout the year.

ESSONNE

ANGERVILLIERS (postal code 91470)
Antiquaire d'Angervilliers 15 Grande Rue.*
Tel. 64 59 02 09.

AUVERS-SAINT-GEORGES (postal code 91580)
Martinière (La) à la Martinière, 1 km. 500 d'Etréchy.*
Tel. 60 80 34 45.

BRUNOY (postal code 91800)
Antiquités de l'Hostellerie 18 rue Dupont Chaumont.
Tel. 60 46 06 07.
Charme d'Antan (Au) 12 rue Montmartel.*
Tel. 60 46 44 25.

BURES-SUR-YVETTE (postal code 91440)
Aupy 27 bis avenue Maréchal Foch.*
Tel. 69 07 72 13.

CHALOU-MOULINEUX (postal code 91740)
Sardon 3 voie des Hospitaliers.*
Tel. 64 95 91 04.

CORBEIL-ESSONNES (postal code 91100)
Antiquité Brocante Didier 9 rue aux Tisseurs.*
Tel. 60 88 46 05.
Quartiers de France (Aux) 44–46 rue Féray.*
Tel. 64 96 36 60.

DOURDAN (postal code 91410)
Ceccaldi 8 avenue Emile Zola.*
Huet 54 rue de Chartres.*
Tel. 64 59 70 13.
Rossignol 9 rue Michel.
Tel. 64 59 73 43 (A).

ETAMPES (postal code 91150)
André 11–13 avenue de la Libération.*
Tel. 64 94 49 32.
Montagnac 2 bis rue Louis Moreau.*
Tel. 64 94 74 70.

FERTE-ALAIS (LA) (postal code 91590)

GIF-SUR-YVETTE (postal code 91190)

Lebreton 21 Résidence de Courcelles.
Tel. 69 28 25 39.
Tarasque (La) 1 square de la Mairie.
Tel. 69 28 44 59.

JANVRY (postal code 91640)
Antiquités à la Ferme Hameau de la Brosse.
Tel. 60 12 08 87

JUVISY (postal code 91260)
Robert 26 rue Biazy.*
Tel. 69 21 79 54

LIMOURS (postal code 91470)
Carrette 6 rue des Concessions.
Martin 5 place Aristide Briand.
Tel. 64 91 23 96 (AB).

LINAS (postal code 91310)
Bresan 12 rue de la Lampe.*
Tel. 69 01 34 48.

LONGJUMEAU (postal code 91160)
Malle Poste 2 bis rue du Général Leclerc.
Tel. 64 48 65 09

MENNECY (postal code 91540)
Atelier d'Art Rustique 2 rue des Châtriés.*
Tel. 64 57 34 32.

MEREVILLE (postal code 91660)
Morgand-Saget 8 et 9 rue Curie.
Tel. 64 95 10 16.

MILLY (postal code 91490)
Aurelia 24 place du Marché.
Tel. 64 24 54 92.
Lebeau 12 rue Langlois.
Tel. 64 98 74 10.
Sirènes (Les) 2 rue Saint-Wulfran.
Tel. 64 98 85 65.

MONTLHERY (postal code 91310)
Aiguière de Cuivre (l') 37 route d'Orléans.
Tel. 69 01 01 03.

RIS-ORANGIS (postal code 91130)
Centre des Occasions 34 rue de la Fontaine.
Tel. 69 25 84 51.
Housselle 3 place de la Gare.
Tel. 69 43 50 57

SAINT-PIERRE-DU-PERRAY (postal code 91100)
Daniel 7 quai des Platanes.
Tel. 60 75 64 05.

SAINT-SULPICE-DE-FAVIERES (postal code 91910)
Causse 7 rue aux Fèves.
Tel. 64 58 62 97.

SAINT-VRAIN (postal code 91770)
Passe Rose (Au) 6 place de l'Eglise.
Tel. 64 56 08 11.

SAVIGNY-SUR-ORGE (postal code 91600)
Jeanne Elise d'Antan 8 place Beaumarchais.
Tel. 69 44 07 77.
Peyronny 10 Grande Rue.*
Trésors de Benett (Les) 52 boulevard Aristide Briand.
Tel. 69 96 15 67.

VIGNEUX (postal code 91270)
Safone 30 rue de la Liberté.*
Tel. 69 42 02 62.

VILLEBON (postal code 91120)
Maison 6 avenue du Val d'Yvette.

VIRY-CHATILLON (postal code 91170)
Jouet 2 avenue de Gaulle.*
Tel. 69 44 18 40.

YERRES (postal code 91330)
Rives de l'Yerres (Les) 2 rue Pierre de Coubertin.
Tel. 69 48 97 42.

HAUTS-DE-SEINE

ANTONY (postal code 92160)
Croisée des Temps (La) 80 avenue Aristide Briand.*
Tel. 42 37 44 17.

BAGNEUX (postal code 92220)
Petit 4 rue des Prés.
Tel. 46 65 37 17.

BOIS-COLOMBES (postal code 92270)
Belle Epoque (La) 16 rue Mertens.*
Tel. 47 80 99 41.
Fil des Ans (Au) 5 rue Victor Hugo.
Tel. 47 84 35 37.
Fleuret 63 rue Charles Duflos.
Tel. 42 42 52 38.
Grout 5 rue Victor Hugo.*
Tel. 42 42 24 16.
Lule 11–17 rue du Général Leclerc.*

BOULOGNE (postal code 92100)
Antiquaire de Boulogne (l') 4 rue Fessart.*
Tel. 46 05 27 80.
Arestyl 66 rue Saussière.
Tel. 46 04 74 43.
Beliah 3 avenue André Morizet.
Tel. 48 25 10 85.
Bennazar 14 rue Gallieni.
Tel. 46 09 10 18.
Gillet 8 bis rue Traversière.*
Lelief 12 rue Mollien.
Tel. 48 25 12 81.
Passé Simple (Le) 14 avenue du Mal de Lattre de Tassigny.*
Poliakoff 80 rue des Tilleuls.*
Tel. 46 05 28 09.

Reflets d'Antan 42 avenue du Général Leclerc.*
Tel. 46 04 28 44.

Style et Ancien 213 boulevard Jean Jaurès.
Tel. 49 10 90 06.

BOURG-LA-REINE (postal code 92340)

Fraize 67 avenue Général Leclerc.
Tel. 46 61 33 06.

CHATILLON-SOUS-BAGNEUX (postal code 92320)

Banewitz 71 boulevard Vanves.
Tel. 46 45 19 45.

CHAVILLE (postal code 92370)

Renouf 546–564 avenue Roger Salengro.*

CLAMART (postal code 92140)

Tanagra 15 rue Hébert.*
Tel. 46 45 05 42.

CLICHY (postal code 92110)

Art et Décoration 13 et 15 impasse Abel Varet.
Tel. 47 37 48 85.

COLOMBES (postal code 92700)

Rochas 36 rue Gabriel Péri.
Tel. 42 42 03 02.

Sonnet 56 rue Pierre Geofroix.*
Tel. 47 81 91 25.

COURBEVOIE (postal code 92400)

Chevalier 64 boulevard Mission-Marchand.*
Tel. 47 88 41 41.

GARCHES (postal code 92380)

Charles 14 avenue Maréchal Leclerc.
Tel. 47 01 12 27.

GARENNE-COLOMBES (LA) (postal code 92250)

Cambon 74 bis boulevard de la République.*
Tel. 42 42 84 28.

ISSY-LES-MOULINEAUX (postal code 92130)

Notre-Dame (Galerie) 7 rue du Gué.
Tel. 47 08 51 67.

LEVALLOIS-PERRET (postal code 92300)

Lamarre "Arte Viva" 25 rue des Trébois.
Tel. 47 37 66 37.

Lemarinier 66 rue Louise Michel.
Tel. 47 37 13 27.

Peretz 1 rue Raspail.*
Tel. 47 39 32 87.

Williams 46 rue Anatole France.
Tel. 47 58 60 11.

MALAKOFF (postal code 92240)

Charles 17 rue Legrand.*
Tel. 42 53 36 08.

MARNES-LA-COQUETTE (postal code 92430)

Bordes 2 place de la Mairie.*
Tel. 47 41 08 32.

Dey 8 bis rue Schlumberger.*
Tel. 47 41 65 31.

Ducomey-Vitry 8 place de la Mairie.*
Tel. 47 41 06 28.

MEUDON (postal code 92190)

Renaudin 48 route des Gardes.*
Tel. 46 26 62 82.

Setruk 23 boulevard des Nations-Unies.*
Tel. 45 07 20 30.

MONTROUGE (postal code 92120)

Amarante 22 rue Gabriel Peri.
Tel. 46 57 88 24.

Bric à Brac 31 rue Racine.*
Tel. 42 53 63 86.

Delotte 50 avenue de la République.
Tel. 42 53 02 66.

Entrepôt Racine 31 rue Racine.
Tel. 46 55 23 19.

NANTERRE (postal code 92000)

Baudet 33 rue Pascal.*

La Source aux Trouvailles 77 avenue Georges Clemenceau.*
Tel. 47 24 11 49.

NEUILLY (postal code 92200)

Arnoux 40 rue des Poissonniers.
Tel. 46 37 04 44.

Art Conseil Elysées 45 avenue Charles de Gaulle.*

Bacchanales Antiquités Autour du Vin et de la Table (Les) 28 rue d'Orléans.*
Tel. 47 38 66 15.

Bical-Lydia 31 rue de Chartres.**
Tel. 46 24 14 30.

Eram 177 avenue Achille Peretti.

Guitine 38 avenue du Roule.*

Larousse-Trombetta 154 avenue Charles de Gaulle.
Tel. 47 22 40 81.

L'Aléors 158 avenue Charles de Gaulle.
Tel. 46 24 10 70.

PUTEAUX (postal code 92800)

Antiquités 96 96 rue Jean Jaurès.*
Tel. 47 73 81 95.

RUEIL-MALMAISON (postal code 92500)

Brocante Rustique (La) 6 rue des Graviers.*
Tel. 47 51 80 38.

Marché Bonaparte (20 dealers) 17 rue de la Libération.
Tel. 47 51 70 85.

Pascaline 2 rue de la Réunion.
Tel. 47 51 39 44.

Vieux Décor (Au) 7 avenue de la République.
Tel. 47 49 67 84.

SAINT-CLOUD (postal code 92210)

Charme du Passé (Au) 56 rue Gounod.*
Tel. 46 02 50 91.

Nina Kaminzer 19 rue Gounod.
Tel. 46 02 33 89.

Roustan 190 boulevard de la République.*

SCEAUX (postal code 92330)

Florian (Galerie) 3 rue Florian.
Tel. 46 61 54 10.

SURESNES (postal code 92150)

Sevene 56 boulevard Henri Sellier.
Tel. 45 06 34 13.

VANVES (postal code 92170)

Markovic 45 rue Jean Bleuzon.
Tel. 47 36 97 54.

Passé Simple (Le) 9 avenue Victor Hugo.
Tel. 46 38 18 54.

VAUCRESSON (postal code 92420)

Dutheil 43 Ancien chemin de l'Empereur.*

Greniers du Butard 38 allée du Butard.
Tel. 47 41 16 12.

Perrot 11 bis rue de la Folie.
Tel. 47 41 39 17.

VILLE-D'AVRAY (postal code 92410)

Dimanche à la Campagne (Un) 52 rue de Saint-Cloud.
Tel. 47 50 24 85.

Tempera 26 rue de Saint-Cloud.
Tel. 47 09 12 98.

OISE

BALAGNY-SUR-THERAIN (postal code 60250)

Rouselle 6 place Gabriel Peri.
Tel. 44 26 43 29.

CAUVIGNY (postal code 60730)

Têtard (François) Chapelle de Château Rouge.
Tel. 44 07 38 37.

CHANTILLY (postal code 60500)

Capler 106 rue de Connétable.
Tel. 44 57 01 88.

Saugue 19 bis rue de Connétable.
Tel. 44 57 05 99.

OGNON (postal code 60810)

Joly 2 route de Senlis.
Tel. 44 54 40 37.

SENLIS (postal code 60301)

Formanoir 7 place Notre-Dame.
Tel. 44 53 10 59.

SEINE-ET-MARNE

BARBIZON (postal code 77630)

Barbizonnaise (La) 79 rue Grande.
Tel. 60 66 27 60.

Chambon 83 rue Grande.
Tel. 60 66 43 55.

Grange (La) 8 rue du 23-Août.
Tel. 60 66 45 32.

BOURRON-MARLOTTE (postal code 77780)

Antiquités du Parvis 30 rue Général de Gaulle.*
Tel. 64 45 94 59; 64 45 79 00.

Jaba, Brocante du Pavé du Roy 9 route N7.

Merklen "Le Pavé Du Roy."
Tel. 64 45 96 18.

Ruffin place Paix.
Tel. 64 45 92 73.

BRIE-COMTE-ROBERT (postal code 77170)

Bonnefoy 3 rue des Cèdres Bleus.*
Tel. 64 05 13 92.

Laetitia (Galerie) 42 rue Général Leclerc.
Tel. 64 05 01 18.

Mulsant (Yves) 29 rue de l'Eglise.*
Tel. 64 05 02 04.

CHAPELLE-LA-REINE (LA) (postal code 77760)

Chambon 2 avenue de Fontainebleau.
Tel. 64 24 33 43.

CHELLES (postal code 77500)

Anne et Dan 21 bis avenue Louvois.
Tel. 60 08 33 14.

COULOMMIERS (postal code 77120)

Ede La Belle Croix, route N34.*
Tel. 84 03 08 87.

COURTIN-LE-BAS (postal code 77650)

Loué 11 rue de Trainel.*

FERTE-SOUS-JOUARRE (LA)
(postal code 77260)

Leglaive 31 avenue Franklin D.
Roosevelt.*
Tel. 60 22 08 42.

FONTAINEBLEAU (postal code
77300)

Ducre 2 rue des Pins, place de la
République.*
Tel. 64 22 04 54.

Félix-Bost-Orthan 57 rue de
France.*
Tel. 64 22 42 35; 62 22 08 54.

Hassler 5 rue de la Cloche.*
Tel. 64 22 34 68.

Hotel des Ventes (Auction House)
5 rue Royale, place du Château.
Tel. 54 22 27 68.
Auctions Friday and Sunday.

Mendels 29 rue Grande.
Tel. 64 22 20 20.

Polowski 16 rue de la Cloche.*

Rest'or 88 rue Aristide Briand.*
Tel. 64 22 74 31.

Thierry May 213 rue Saint-
Merry.*
Tel. 64 22 05 46.

Tic et Tac (Au) 44 rue de France.
Tel. 64 22 17 62.

GUERMANTES (postal code
77400)

Deux Châteaux (Les)
(B. Hamelin) 79 avenue des
Deux-Châteaux.
Tel. 60 07 83 05.

ISLES-LES-VILLENOY (postal code
77450)

Grand Portail Antiquités (Le)
77 rue de Meaux.*
Tel. 60 04 43 89.

JOSSIGNY (postal code 77400)

Ridard 2 rue de Tournan.*
Tel. 64 02 24 80.

LAGNY (postal code 77400)

Coremales Matériaux de Jadis
35 quai du Pré-Long.
Tel. 64 30 02 36; 64 30 26 46.

MEAUX (postal code 77100)

Brojou 1 avenue Maréchal Joffre.
Tel. 64 34 06 89.

Vasseur 13 rue de la
Cordonnerie.
Tel. 64 34 08 93.

MELUN (postal code 77000)

7 (Galerie) 7 rue Guy Baudoin.
Tel. 64 39 98 21.

Brakha 32 rue du Général de
Gaulle.*
Tel. 64 52 30 45.

Brocante Saint-Ambroise 2 rue
Saint-Ambroise.*
Tel. 64 39 61 11.

Cottage (Le) 3 avenue de Meaux.
Tel. 64 52 16 47.

MONTEREAU (postal code 77130)

Antiquités-Brocante 15 rue Alexis
Petit.
Tel. 64 32 91 32.

MONTRY (postal code 77450)

Alfred Valette (Montry Style)
47 avenue du 27-Août 1944.*
Tel. 60 04 01 77.

MORET-SUR-LOING (postal code
77250)

Hassler 39 rue Grande.*
Tel. 60 70 14 95; 84 45 96 97.

PROVINS (postal code 77160)

Antiquaire (l') 38 rue de
Changis.*
Tel. 64 00 07 74.

Miguaise 12 rue Friperie and 19
avenue de la Libération.
Tel. 64 00 62 55.

SABLONNIERES (postal code
77510)

Château Morin Antiquités.*
Tel. 64 04 90 49.

URY (postal code 77116)

Anne Leonard Diffusion 20 rue de
Nemours.
Tel. 64 24 47 17.

VERNOU-SUR-SEINE (postal code
77670)

Moulin du Bois (Le) à la Basse-
Roche chemin du Moulin-des-
Serpes.*
Tel. 64 32 21 20.

SEINE-SAINT-DENIS

AUBERVILLIERS (postal code
93300)

Dupuis 62 avenue de la
République.
Tel. 48 33 29 00.

AULNAY-SOUS-BOIS (postal code
93600)

Bonheur du Jour (Au) 61 rue
Dupuis.*

Decary 5 rue Maxime Gorki.*

Waintrob 61 rue Anatole France.

BAGNOLET (postal code 93170)

Cavallazzi 40 rue des Pernelles.*

BLANC-MESNIL (LE) (postal code
93150)

Gombert 2 rue Corot.
Tel. 48 67 29 67.

Tapisseries de France 17 rue
Laennec.
Tel. 48 67 68 13.

EPINAY-SUR-SEINE (postal code
93800)

Greenwich 116 rue de Paris.
Tel. 48 27 80 44.

Petit et Simon 197 avenue
d'Enghien.

GAGNY (postal code 93220)

Mayfair Tradition 12 rue Aristide
Briand.
Tel. 43 81 41 72.

LES LILAS (postal code 93260)

Mars (Galerie de) 98 avenue
Pasteur.

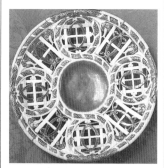

MONTFERMEIL (postal code
93370)

Broc'Antique 2 rue des Moulins.
Tel. 43 30 45 71.

MONTREUIL (postal code 93100)

Fouine à Deux Têtes (La) 8 bis
rue Beaumarchais.
Tel. 48 59 30 06.

Marché aux Puces Saturday
through Monday.

NEUILLY-PLAISANCE (postal code
93360)

Dépôt-Vente 15 avenue du
Maréchal-Foch.
Tel. 43 09 84 00.

NOISY-LE-GRAND (postal code
93160)

Brocante de Noisy (La) 7 rue de
la République.
Tel. 43 03 77 73.

PANTIN (postal code 93500)

Uriet 3 rue Ernest Renan.*

PAVILLONS-SOUS-BOIS (LES)
(postal code 93320)

Petite Brocante (La) 172 avenue
Aristide Briand.
Tel. 48 48 40 16.

PRE-SAINT-GERVAIS (LE) (postal
code 93310)

Theaux 24 rue Garibaldi.*
Tel. 48 46 57 69.

RAINCY (LE) (postal code 93340)

Richard 2 bis allée des Maisons
Russes.
Tel. 43 02 76 33.

Trianon Antiquités 5 rond-point
de Mottemeil.*
Tel. 43 01 97 38.

ROSNY-SOUS-BOIS (postal code
93110)

Meubles d'Occasion 14 rue
Richard Garnier.*
Tel. 48 55 95 90.

SAINT-DENIS (postal code 93200)

Daumal 20 rue Catulienne.*
Tel. 42 43 60 24.

Deligny 36 rue du Bailly.*
Tel. 48 20 99 97.

VAL-DE-MARNE

ALFORTVILLE (postal code
94140)

Antiquités Vonthron 164 rue P.
Vaillant-Cou.
Tel. 43 75 16 74.

Ledot-Weil 12 rue des Camélias.
Tel 43 78 17 00.

BONNEUIL-SUR-MARNE (postal
code 94300)

Grenier de Mère-Grand (Au) 42
rue Victor Hugo.
Tel. 43 39 40 97.

CHARENTON (postal code 94220)

Carcanade 15 route de Paris.
Tel. 43 78 70 74.

Présents du Passé (Aux) 44 rue de
Paris.*
Tel. 43 76 83 44.

Theriaques (Galerie des) 2 rue de
l'Embarcadère.
Tel. 43 76 18 73.

Vanhoutte 166 rue de Paris.
Tel. 43 68 62 49

CHOISY-LE-ROI (postal code
94600)

Epoque 33 avenue Anatole
France.
Tel. 48 64 75 96.

FONTENAY (postal code 94120)

Bernard 2 rue de la Réunion.
Tel. 48 73 73 40.

GENTILLY (postal code 94250)

Vachon Antiquités 131 avenue
P. V. Couturier.
Tel. 47 35 26 30.

JOINVILLE (postal code 94340)

Tamburrini 8 rue Lefèvre.*

MAISONS-ALFORT (postal code
94700)

Gavotti 129 rue de Normandie.*

NOGENT-SUR-MARNE (postal code
94130)

Cendrillon 10 place Pierre
Semard.
Tel. 48 77 09 93.

Ile Aux Trésors 75 grande rue
Charles de Gaulle.*
Tel. 48 73 75 02.

Maître Allain 162 grande rue
Charles de Gaulle.
Tel. 48 71 06 10.

Quinsier 171 grande rue Charles
de Gaulle.*
Tel. 48 71 03 29.

PERREUX (LE) (postal code
94170)

Deletrain 207 avenue du Général
de Gaulle.*
Tel. 48 72 91 95.

SAINT-MANDE (postal code
94160)

Berson 17 avenue Quihou.
Tel. 48 08 66 60.

Ferment 3 rue de l'Epinette.
Tel. 48 08 48 77.
By appointment only.

SAINT-MAUR (postal code 94100)

Lambert 28 bis rue Vassal.*

SAINT-MAURICE (postal code
94410)

Bâtique France 126 rue du
Maréchal Leclerc.
Tel. 43 68 55 77.

SUCY-EN-BRIE (postal code 94370)
Julien 9 rue Maurice Berteaux.
Tel. 49 82 45 10.

VARENNE-SAINT-HILAIRE (LA) (postal code 94210)
Athena (Galerie) 27 avenue du Bac.
Tel. 43 97 18 59.
Decaix 8 rue Elisée-Reclus.*
Olim 85 rue La Fayette.
Tel. 48 83 66 17.
Temps Jadis (Au) 43 avenue du Bac.
Tel. 48 89 15 50.

VILLEJUIF (postal code 94800)
Laurient's 14 bis boulevard Gorki.
Mamann 123b–125 rue Ambroise Croizat.*
Tel. 47 26 21 41.
R.S.M. 90 avenue de Paris.
Tel. 47 26 20 00.

VILLENEUVE-SAINT-GEORGES (postal code 94190)
Monard 43 rue de Crosne.
Tel. 43 89 06 80.

VILLIERS-SUR-MARNE (postal code 94350)
Iris Blanc (l') 5 route de Combault.*
Tel. 43 04 51 70.

VINCENNES (postal code 94300)
Belle Brocante 35 rue Massuc.
Tel. 43 98 31 02.
Delage 16 bis rue Charles Silvestri.*

Grillon (Le) 5 rue Lejemptel.**
Tel. 43 28 26 30.
Lerisse 35 rue Massue.
Tel. 43 98 31 02.
Mouchet 29 rue Raymond du Temple.
Tel. 43 74 36 63.
Pinguet 2 rue Jean Moulin.
Tel. 43 74 89 49.

VITRY-SUR-SEINE (postal code 94400)
Boyer 84 rue Edith Cavell.*

VAL-D'OISE

AMBLEVILLE (postal code 95710)
Barbier Ferme d'en Bas.
Tel. 34 67 73 56.

ARGENTEUIL (postal code 95100)
Clementi 6 rue Defresne Bast.*

Salle des Ventes du Val Notre-Dame 86 route de Pontoise.
Tel. 39 80 31 00.

ASNIERES-SUR-OISE (postal code 95270)
Grenier de l'Abbaye (Le) 8 Grande Rue.
Tel. 30 35 39 30.

AUVERS-SUR-OISE (postal code 95430)
Cruveillier 27 rue François Villon.
Tel. 30 36 14 66.

BEAUCHAMP (postal code 95250)
Lange 177 chaussée Jules César.
Tel. 39 60 94 65.
Maison Gilles 19 avenue Pierre Semard.
Tel. 39 95 42 19.

BEAUMONT-SUR-OISE (postal code 95260)
Khormaian place de la Mairie.
Tel. 34 69 28 09.
Malle Ancienne (La) 12 rue Nationale.
Tel. 34 70 40 80.

CORMEILLES (postal code 95240)
Château d'Or 87 boulevard Clemenceau.
Tel. 34 50 07 84.
Lente 127 rue Gabriel Peri.*
Tel. 39 78 73 92.

DEUIL-LA-BARRE (postal code 95170)
Bocquillon 37 avenue Division Leclerc.
Tel. 39 83 27 71.

EAUBONNE (postal code 95600)
James 20 rue Stéphane Proust.
Tel. 39 59 55 36.

ECOUEN (postal code 95440)
Mateo-Albaladejo 4 rue Emmanuel Duverger.*

ENGHIEN-LES-BAINS (postal code 95880)
Antiquités Serry 3 boulevard du Lac.*
Tel. 34 12 27 14.
Armand 183 avenue de la Division-Leclerc.
Tel. 39 64 12 34.
Cheyrouze 2 rue de Mora.*
Tel. 34 12 86 18.
English Antiques 9 rue du Général de Gaulle.
Tel. 34 17 53 49.
Vaugeois 86 rue de Départ.*

FRANCONVILLE (postal code 95130)
Sam Antiquités 68 rue du Plessis.
Tel. 34 13 60 62.

FRETTE-SUR-SEINE (LA) (postal code 95530)
Schaefer 10 Résidence bord de Seine.*
Tel. 39 78 20 94.

GOUSSAINVILLE (postal code 95190)
Beauvoir (De) 27 rue Brûlée.
Tel. 39 92 86 70.

GRISY-LES-PLATRES (postal code 95810)
Grisy-Pomme 18 rue Général de Gaulle.
Tel. 34 66 66 88.

HEROUVILLE (postal code 95300)
Bergerie (La) 2 rue Georges Duhamel.*
Tel. 34 66 52 23.

ISLE-ADAM (l') (postal code 95290)
Duval 3 rue de Nogent.
Tel. 34 69 09 97.

LOUVRES (postal code 95380)
Baron 29 rue de Paris.*
Tel. 34 68 10 14.

MAGNY-EN-VEXIN (postal code 95420)
Clo 53 rue de Paris.
Tel. 34 67 04 05.
Fraysse (Geneviève) 27 place d'Armes.
Tel. 34 67 03 15.
Jallier 9 bis rue de Crosne.
Tel. 34 67 11 26.

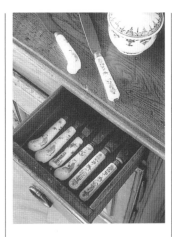

Lechauguette 52 rue de Rouen.
Tel. 34 67 00 09.
Ratinaud 6 rue de Crosne.
Tel. 34 67 19 28.

MERY-SUR-OISE (postal code 95540)
Beurville 49 and 60 rue Marcel Perrin.
Tel. 30 36 65 89.
Caves de Mery (Les) 40 avenue Marcel Perrin.
Tel. 30 36 40 22.
Touren 11 route de Pontoise, La Bonneville.
Tel. 39 58 35 63.

MONTMORENCY (postal code 95160)
Beauvais 8 rue du Docteur Demirieau.*
Tel. 39 64 24 02.

NUCOURT (postal code 95420)
Gribinski 2 rue de l'Arche.
Tel. 34 67 43 98.

PONTOISE (postal code 95300)
Taillandier 4 rue de la Bretonnerie.
Tel. 30 38 16 40.
Village des Antiquaires 1 ancienne route de Rouen.
Tel. 30 32 12 22.

PUISEUX (postal code 95650)
Grange aux Meubles (La) les jardins de Cergy-Pontoise.
Tel. 34 42 12 31.

ROCHE-GUYON (LA) (postal code 95780)
Antiquités du Château (Les) place de la Mairie.
Tel. 34 79 74 75.
Beaufort 18 rue du Général Leclerc.*
Tel. 34 79 73 31.

SANNOIS (postal code 95110)
Bouillotte (La) 2 boulevard Charles de Gaulle.*
Tel. 34 10 31 02.
Maja Antiquités 58 boulevard Charles de Gaulle.*
Tel. 34 10 07 61.

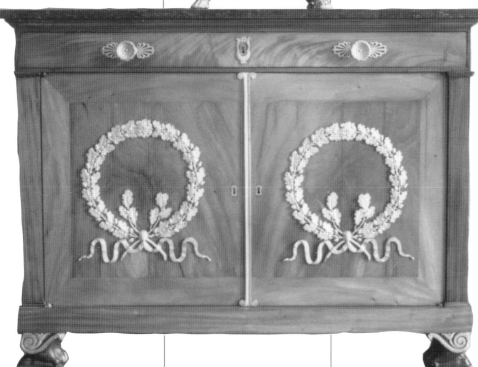

YVELINES

ABLIS (postal code 78660).
Hannoyer 2 rue de la Mairie.
Tel. 30 59 11 10.

ACHERES (postal code 78260)
Souedet-Beys 1 avenue Maurice Berteaux.
Tel. 39 11 08 00.

BAILLY (postal code 78870)
Antiquités et Décoration Bailly 26 route Maule.
Tel. 34 62 62 12.

BAZAINVILLE (postal code 78550)
Quitard 48 route de Paris.*
Tel. 34 87 61 88.

BAZOCHES-SUR-GUYONNE (postal code 78490)
Leca Rosemania Houjarray.
Tel. 34 86 04 39.

BENNECOURT (postal code 78270)
Marchal au Hameau de Tripleval.*
Tel. 30 93 01 49.

BOUGIVAL (postal code 78380)
Pelzer 4 rue Général Leclerc.*
Tel. 39 69 08 57.

Pennau 14 quai Rennequin.
Tel. 39 18 05 41.

CARRIERES-SUR-SEINE (postal code 78420)
Blondel 68 route de Chatou.*
Tel. 39 14 39 63.

CELLE-SAINT-CLOUD (postal code 78170)
Fichet 28 avenue de Verdun.
Tel. 39 18 14 46.

Jackie Antiquités 42 avenue de la Jonchère.
Tel. 39 18 33 67.

Lefebvre 15 rue Mauge.

CHAMBOURCY (postal code 78240)

Galienne 15 chemin de la Gâtine.*

Legoffe 22 route Mantes.
Tel. 39 65 33 32.

CHANTELOUP-LES-VIGNES (postal code 78570)
Dume 20 impasse Vincent Barrois.
Tel. 39 70 75 80.

CHATOU (postal code 78400)
Lenoir 42 rue Cormmier.
Tel. 34 80 63 21.

CHAVENAY (postal code 78450)
Boissan 38 Grande-Rue.*
Tel. 30 54 32 24.

CHESNAY (LE) (postal code 78150)
Antiquités de Parly (Sainte Odile Theaux)
9 avenue Dutartre, Parly II.
Tel. 39 55 07 08.

Barilleau 13 rue Docteur Audigier.
Tel. 39 55 13 12.

Lebrun 70 rue de Versailles.*
Tel. 39 54 25 76.

CHEVREUSE (postal code 78460)
Antiquités 10 rue Lalande.
Beauvillard 30 rue Porte de Paris.
Tel. 30 52 16 58.

Kerjolis 9 rue Lalande.
Tel. 30 52 94 92.

Vieux Chevreuse (Au) 16 bis rue Lalande.
Tel. 30 52 07 31.

COIGNIERES (postal code 78310)
Domaine Particulier rue Pont des Landes.
Tel. 34 61 64 82.

Tiphaine rue des Broderies.
Tel. 34 61 24 25.

CONDE-SUR-VESGRE (postal code 78113)
Bouquet Jacoillot place de l'Eglise.*
Tel. 34 87 04 64.

CONFLANS-SAINTE-HONORINE (postal code 78700)
Brocstore 52 rue Désiré Clément.
Tel. 39 72 68 84.

Forfait 3 boulevard Troussel.

Juin 8 rue Anglais.
Tel. 39 19 99 49.

Pinchon 219 avenue Carnot.*

CRAVENT (postal code 78270)
Chenuet 1 rue André Mojard.*

CRESPIERES (postal code 78290)
Kohn 5 rue du Pasteur Logé.
Tel. 30 54 50 49.

CROISSY-SUR-SEINE (postal code 78290)
Detheve 4 allée Capucines.
Tel. 39 76 98 93.

Erico.
Tel. 39 76 67 08.

Pouliot 39 boulevard Fernand Hostachy.
Tel. 39 76 22 00.

DAMPIERRE (postal code 78720)
Barre 3 place Eglise.
Tel. 30 52 54 26.

ELANCOURT (postal code 78990)
Gervais 5 rue de Laon.

ESSARTS-LE-ROI (postal code 78690)
Antiquaire du Bâtiment (l') à Saint-Hubert 58 rue de la Haie-aux-Vaches.
Tel. 34 84 98 83.

Choquer 2 rue Georges Pompidou.
Tel. 30 41 51 38.

FOURQUEUX (postal code 78112)
Légende des Siècles (La) 3 rue Saint-Germain.
Tel. 34 51 86 07.

GAMBAIS (postal code 78950)
Leda-Décors 27 rue de Goupigny.*
Tel. 34 87 02 32; 34 87 07 16.

Letellier 131 rue des Novales.*
Tel. 34 87 01 66.

HOUDAN (postal code 78550)
Antiquités Brocante de la Tour 23 rue Enclos.
Tel. 30 59 73 66.

Ballan 34 rue d'Epernon.*
Tel. 30 59 70 88.

Hier à Aujourdhui (d') 7 rue Saint-Mathieu.*
Tel. 30 59 72 72.

Pierres d'Antan Michel Roger Lieudit "La Forêt" route N12.
Tel. 30 58 72 77.

HOUILLES (postal code 78800)
Greniers Français (Les) 136 boulevard Jean Jaurès.
Tel. 39 13 75 86.

Huillier (l') 18 rue Gabriel Peri.
Tel. 39 68 94 50.

Meubles Anciens 96 boulevard Jean Jaurès.
Tel. 39 68 11 84.

Peyssard 41 rue Gabriel Peri.
Tel. 39 68 66 68.

Truchelut 22 rue Desaix.
Tel. 39 68 21 00.

JOUY-EN-JOSAS (postal code 78350)
Grenier de Jouy (Le) 3 rue de la Libération.
Tel. 39 56 16 73.

Trepo 61 rue Charles de Gaulle.*

JUZIERS (postal code 78820)
Edenley 178 avenue de Paris.
Tel. 34 75 68 77.

Levecher 16 rue Fontaine.
Tel. 34 75 61 56.

Moulin de la Brocante 92 avenue Nationale.*
Tel. 34 75 60 56.

LIMAY (postal code 78520)
Duron 11 boulevard Aristide Briand.
Tel. 34 77 13 67.

LOMMOYE (postal code 78270)
Saule 1 chemin Melotterie Mesnil Guyon.
Tel. 34 76 11 86.

LOUVECIENNES (postal code 78430)
Louve Ancienne (La) 27 avenue Général Leclerc.
Tel. 39 69 21 07.

MAISONS-LAFFITTE (postal code 78600)
Altazin 55 avenue Général de Gaulle.
Tel. 39 62 31 54.

Grenier des Particuliers (Le) 34 rue Guynemer.
Tel. 39 62 50 00.

Longueville 12 and 21 rue de la Vieille Eglise.*
Tel. 39 62 09 96.

Mylord's 11 avenue Lonqueil.
Tel. 39 62 06 50.

Rivière 78 rue des Côtes.*
Tel. 39 62 02 39.

MARLY-LE-ROI (postal code 78160)

Franc-Sergent (Au) 1 rue Alexandre Dumas.
Tel. 39 58 12 92.

MONDREVILLE (postal code 78980)

Chalvignac 12 rue Nationale.*
Tel. 30 42 52 20.

MONTFORT-L'AMAURY (postal code 78490)

Coville 8 boulevard de la Moutière.*
Tel. 34 86 00 02; 34 86 97 89.
16 place de la Libèration.
Tel. 34 86 97 89.

Dzido 13 rue de Sance.
Tel. 34 86 18 94.

Fallais 28 place Robert.*
Tel. 34 86 02 48.

Hamon 21 rue de Sance.*
Tel. 34 86 02 48.

Morlat 31 rue de Paris.
Tel. 34 86 70 84.

Tran 21 rue Normande.*
Tel. 34 86 03 93.

Turiaf 45 rue de Paris.*
Tel. 34 86 91 80.

MUREAUX (LES) (postal code 78130)

Antiquités-Foch 36 bis avenue Foch.
Tel. 30 99 81 81.

Bibi Broc 123 bis rue Jean Jaurès.*
Tel. 30 99 31 65.

Broc'Antiq 9 rue Paul Doumer.
Tel. 34 74 91 92.

Forceville (de) 13 avenue Près.
Tel. 34 74 96 58.

NEAUPHLE-LE-CHÂTEAU (postal code 78640)

Grenier de Neauphle (Le) 19 rue Saint-Martin.*
Tel. 34 89 09 15.

POISSY (postal code 78300)

Loyer 4 boulevard Deveux.*
Tel. 39 65 09 88.

PONTCHARTRAIN (postal code 78760)

Ferrand 12 route Mousseaux.
Tel. 34 87 80 64.

Grange (La) 13 rue de Coignières.*
Tel. 34 87 83 42.

Landman 3 rue de l'Echiquier.*
Tel. 34 89 02 36.

Tardif 61 route Nationale.*
Tel. 34 89 02 59.

RAMBOUILLET (postal code 78120)

Baudu 21 place Félix Faure (AB).*

SAINT-GERMAIN-EN-LAYE (postal code 78100)

Antiquités Dauphine Maison Susen place Dauphine.
Tel. 34 51 26 76.

Brocéliande 21 rue du Vieil-Abreuvoir.
Tel. 34 51 55 24.

Collections du Passé 5 rue du Vieil-Abreuvoir.
Tel. 34 51 98 12.

Cour de l'Antiquaire (La) 39 rue de Poissy.
Tel. 30 61 24 89.

Dépot-Vente Des Yvelines 54 rue de Paris.
Tel. 34 51 01 33.

Evrard 8 rue des Coches.*
Tel. 34 51 26 87.

Grenier de Margot (Le) 30 rue des Louviers.*
Tel. 39 73 91 50.

Kaji 39 rue de Poissy.
Tel. 30 61 24 89.

Marotte (La) 20 rue Danès de Montardat.
Tel. 30 61 18 10.

Puces de Saint-Germain (Les) 1 rue des Louviers.
Tel. 39 73 66 52.

Sardam-Antiquités 141 rue Léon Desoyer.*
Tel. 39 73 95 02.

VERSAILLES (postal code 78000)

Baily 18–20 rué Royale.*
Tel. 39 50 43 71.

Barbier 38 rue Rémilly.
Tel. 39 50 00 06.

Bejarry (de) 16 passage de la Geôle.
Tel. 39 02 07 67.

Belles Occasions (Aux) (Mme. J. Chevreteau) 79 rue de la Paroisse.*
Tel. 39 50 24 29.

Brocante 4 rue des Deux-Portes.

Brocante de l'Orangerie 33 rue de l'Orangerie.
Tel. 39 50 28 74.

Brocantique (La) 25 rue des Etats-Généraux.
Tel. 39 51 11 92.

Carré de la Fontaine (Le) 63 rue Royale.
Tel. 39 50 07 07.

Carré des Antiquaires passage de la Geôle.
Tel. 39 51 84 96.

Carré des Antiquaires: Baillon (Glie).
Tel. 30 21 40 92.

Carré des Antiquaires: Barilleau Antiquités passage de la Geôle.
Tel. 39 02 07 67.

Carré des Antiquaires: Bivouac (Le).
Tel. 39 49 94 15.

Carré des Antiquaires: Chalvignac passage de la Geôle.
Tel. 39 49 04 80.

Carré des Antiquaires: Cheval Bleu (Le) passage de la Geôle.
Tel. 39 49 48 92.

Carré des Antiquaires: Claude d'Athis passage de la Geôle.
Tel. 39 49 00 88.

Carré des Antiquaires: Cluzel passage de la Geôle.
Tel. 39 49 48 82.

Carré des Antiquaires: Courtioux (du) passage de la Geôle.
Tel. 39 49 01 44; 39 51 57 42.

Carré des Antiquaires: Evasion (l') passage de la Geôle.
Tel. 39 02 77 07.

Carré des Antiquaires: Juliette Antiquités.

Carré des Antiquaires: Katana-Ya passage de la Geôle.
Tel. 39 02 79 79.

Carré des Antiquaires: Leclercq passage de la Geôle.
Tel. 30 21 32 19.

Carré des Antiquaires: Lorenzelli.

Carré des Antiquaires: Lucbert.
Tel. 39 53 47 56.

Carré des Antiquaires: Murisserie (La) passage de la Geôle.
Tel. 39 02 10 28.

Carré des Antiquaires: Saint-Voirin (de) passage de la Geôle.
Tel. 39 50 62 63.

Carré des Antiquaires: Victoria and Mary passage de la Geôle.
Tel. 39 02 77 80.

Caverne des Particuliers (La) 12 rue des Etats-Généraux.
Tel. 30 21 10 43.

Coralie 66 bis rue Royale.
Tel. 39 51 34 23.

Daguenet 3 place Hoche.
Tel. 39 50 67 14.

Davroux Dejean 4 and 8 impasse des Chevau-Légers.*
Tel. 39 53 36 70.

Doxat 7 place Saint-Louis.
Tel. 39 51 71 70.

Epoque (La Galerie de l') 24 rue Baillet Reviron.
Tel. 30 21 89 97.

Gay 2 rue Abbé-de-l'Epée.
Tel. 39 50 12 60.

Grange (La) 13 rue Pourvoierie.
Tel. 39 53 50 31.

Gutman 10 rue Rameau.
Tel. 39 51 30 96.

Hazard 21 and 32 rue des Réservoirs.*
Tel. 39 50 08 78.

Insolite 27 rue Satory.
Tel. 39 50 01 04.

Kerdrain 33 avenue de Saint-Cloud.
Tel. 39 50 64 22.

Lefebvre 38 rue de la Paroisse.
Tel. 39 50 44 84.

Lenoir 4 passage Saladin.
Tel. 39 50 65 63.

Martinaud 39 rue d'Anjou.
Tel. 39 02 06 58.

Montansier (Galerie) (Mme. Mercade) 13 rue de la Paroisse.*
Tel. 39 50 27 96.

Passage des Antiquaires 10 rue Rameau.
Tel. 39 53 84 96.
Passage des Antiquaires: Barilleau-Antiquités 10 rue Rameau.
Tel. 39 53 84 96.
Passage des Antiquaires: Blandices (Les).
Tel. 39 53 84 96.
Passage des Antiquaires: Charmes d'Autrefois (Aux) 10 rue Rameau.
Tel. 39 50 62 92.
Passage des Antiquaires: Couleurs du Temps (Aux) 10 rue Rameau.
Tel. 39 02 09 68.
Passage des Antiquaires: Dubois 10 rue Rameau.
Tel. 39 49 57 64.
Passage des Antiquaires: Eglantier (l') 10 rue Rameau.
Tel. 60 11 01 86.
Passage des Antiquaires: Jantzen 10 rue Rameau.
Tel. 39 51 10 46.
Passage des Antiquaires: Marie Maxime.
Tel. 39 53 84 96.
Passage des Antiquaires: Messageot 10 rue Rameau.
Tel. 39 53 84 96.
Passage des Antiquaires: Ortega 10 rue Rameau.
Tel. 39 02 79 09.
Passage des Antiquaires: Sommertime.
Tel. 39 51 17 60.
Passage des Antiquaires: Suissa-Antiquités 10 rue Rameau.
Tel. 30 21 11 57.
Passage des Antiquaires: Tourmaline 10 rue Rameau.
Tel. 39 02 26 19.
Pellat de Villedon 5 rue du Marché-Neuf.
Tel. 39 51 16 72.
Pouillon 2 rue Menard* and 7 rue des Etats-Généraux.
Tel. 39 51 78 60.

Ravier 23 rue Carnot.
Tel. 39 50 13 74.
Renaissances 15 rue de la Paroisse.*
Tel. 39 51 90 33.
Repaire d'Arcane (Le) 17 rue d'Anjou.
Tel. 39 50 21 08.
Saint-Louis (Galerie) carré de la Fontaine, 11 rue de l'Orient.
Tel. 30 21 54 94.
Servé-Catelin 14 bis rue Baillet-Reviron.
Tel. 39 02 79 79.
Village des Antiquaires 10 rue Rameau.
Tel. 39 53 84 96.
Village des Antiquaires: Barbier 10 rue Rameau.
Tel. 39 53 50 31.
Village des Antiquaires: Choses d'Autrefois 10 rue Rameau.
Village des Antiquaires: Dubois Remy.
Tel. 39 49 57 64.
Village des Antiquaires: Gonther Couture.
Tel. 39 53 41 34.
Village des Antiquaires: Grenier d'Hélène (Le) 10 rue Rameau.
Tel. 39 02 11 56.
Village des Antiquaires: Grenier du Butard (Le).
Tel. 47 41 16 12.
Village des Antiquaires: Leyjour 10 rue Rameau.*
Tel. 39 51 75 53.
Wemaere 1 impasse des Chevau-Légers.*
Tel. 39 50 42 90.

VESINET (LE) (postal code 78110)
Toury 81 boulevard des Etats-Unis.*
Tel. 39 52 03 99.

VILLIERS-LE-MAHIEU (postal code 78770)
Ruspoli "Beaupréau."
Tel. 34 87 41 37.

THE PARIS FLEA MARKET

ST. OUEN (postal code 93400)
Marché Biron entrances on rue des Rosiers and avenue Michelet.
Stand 190 Etendart
Tel. 40 10 15 73.
Stand 156 Lachaud
Tel. 40 12 09 40.
Stand 7 Gaignon
Tel. 40 10 86 81.
Stand 115 Bitoun
Tel. 40 11 96 54.
Stand 199 Bouriquet
Tel. 40 10 23 56.
Stand 51 Heimroth
Tel. 40 11 02 37.
Stand 1 Moufflet
Tel. 40 10 84 09.
Marché Cambo entrance 7 rue Jules Vallès.
Stand Lefèvre
Tel. 40 12 85 04.
Marché Jules Vallès entrance 7 rue Jules Vallès.
Marché Malassis entrance rue des Rosiers and passage Marceau
Stand Humeurs
Stand Couque
Marché Paul Bert entrances on

18 rue Paul Bert and 96, 100 and 102 rue des Rosiers.
Stand 15 Jacquet, Allée 1
Stand 160, 163, 165 Busson, Allée 3
Stand 17 Bachelier, Allée 1
Stand 176 Busson, Allée 4
Stand 233 Humeurs, Allée 5
Stand 259 Humeurs, Allée 5
Stand 36 Letellier, Allée 2
Stand 212 Lévy, Allée 5
Stand 216 Bouchetard, Allée 5
Marché des Rosiers entrance 3, rue Paul Bert.
Marché Serpette entrance 110, rue des Rosiers.
Stand 26, Gosselin, Allée 1.
Tel. 40 10 13 50.
Stand 10, Gribinski, Allée 1
Stand 18, Quitard, Allée 3.
Tel. 40 10 00 24.
Stand 20, Rousseaux, Allée 6
Stands 11–13, Rosenthal, Allée 4.
Tel. 40 11 54 14.
Stand 9, Couque, Allée 2
L'usine entrance 18, rue des Bons Enfants.
See dealers Neveu and Picard.
Marché Vernaison entrance 136, avenue Michelet, and 99 rue des Rosiers.
Stand 141, Giovannoni, Allée 3

PARIS

Autre Jour, 26 avenue de la Bourdonnais, 75007.
Tel. 47 05 36 60.
Bain Marie, Au, 10 rue Boissy d'Anglas, 75008.
Tel. 42 66 59 74.
Bellanger, J., 26 boulevard Saint-Germain, 75007.
Tel. 43 54 39 90.
Boucaud, 24 rue du Cherche-Midi, 75006.
Tel. 42 22 43 54.
Caillat, 24 Faubourg Saint-Antoine, 75012.
Tel. 43 43 92 94.
Courteaux-Enault, 41 rue Saint-André-des-Arts, 75006.
France de Forceville, 17 rue de la Grange-Batelière, 75009.
Tel. 40 22 07 08.
Gayet, Anne, 3 rue de Luynes, 75007.
Tel. 45 44 79 85.
Haga, 22 rue de Grenelle, 75007.
Tel. 42 22 82 40.
Huillier, l', 42 rue de Verneuil, 75007.
Tel. 42 60 23 03.
Louvre des Antiquaires (250 dealers), 2 place du Palais Royal, 75001.
Tel. 42 97 27 00.
Maillard, Colin, 11 rue Miromesnil, 75008.
Tel. 42 65 43 62.
Perrin, 98 rue du Faubourg Saint-Honoré, 75008.
Tel. 42 65 01 38.
Ratton Ladnière, 14 rue de Marignan, 75008.
Tel. 43 59 58 21.
Rullier, 34 rue de Lille, 75007.
Tel. 42 61 15 47.
Village Suisse, 78 avenue de Suffren, 75015.
    Marchand d'Oublié, Stand 19, Tel. 43 06 84 41.
    Daniel, Christine, Stand 32, Tel. 45 67 59 55.
    Nguyen, Céline, Stand 6, Tel. 45 67 39 55.
Vincent, Anne, 31 boulevard Raspail, 75007.
Tel. 40 49 02 21.

RESTORERS

Tapestry restoration: Magy Bocquet, 7 route Nationale,

60300 Chamant,
Tel. (16) 44 53 39 94.
Faience restoration: Mademoiselle Biget, 8 rue Lalo, 75116 Paris, Tel. 45 00 20 53.

ILE-DE-FRANCE PAINTERS

Auner, 13 bis rue de Grenelle, 75007 Paris, Tel. 45 66 91 08.

Bernard, Blaise, (sculptor), Maillebois, Tel. 37 48 15 03.

Lernoud, Christian, Apremont, Tel. 44 25 47 35.

Millasson, 6 square Copernic, Résidence Iena, 78150 Le Chesnay Tel. 39 55 01 41.

Ramuntcho de Saint-Amand, Chatou, Tel. 30 71 47 92.

ANTIQUES FAIRS AND MARKETS

(Most of these events fall into three categories: a *marché aux puces*—a flea market—or a *foire à la brocante*—a bric-à-brac fair—both of which offer an assortment of antiques, knickknacks and secondhand goods; or a *salon des antiquaires*—an antiques show—where the highest quality goods are usually found.)

Argenteuil: Marché aux Puces, every Sunday morning.

Asnières-sur-Oise: (Royaumont), Salon des Antiquaires, Easter weekend.

Barbizon: Foire à la Brocante, fourth Sunday of April.

Chatou: Foire à la Brocante et aux Jambons, 10 days in early March and 10 days at the end of September.

Corbeil-Essonnes: Foire à la Brocante, allée Aristide Briand, Thursday of Ascension Week.

Dourdan: Foire à la Brocante, December.

Enghien-les-Bains: Salon des Antiquaires, last weekend in January.

La Ferté-Alais: Foire à la Brocante, weekend closest to November 11.

La Ferté-Gaucher: Foire à la Brocante, around June 20.

Magny-en-Vexin: Salon des Antiquaires, weekend of Pentecost.

Maisons-Laffitte: Exposition des Antiquaires, second weekend of September.

Meaux: Marché aux Puces, last Sunday of every month.

Milly-la-Forêt: Foire à la Brocante, second weekend in March.

Moret-sur-Loing: Foire à la Brocante, first weekend in September.

Provins: Foire à la Brocante, last weekend in January.
Marché aux Puces, third Sunday of every month except during the winter.

Samois-sur-Seine: Marché aux Puces, last Sunday of May, June, July, August, September, and October.

Savigny-sur-Orge: Marché aux Puces, first Saturday and second Sunday of every month.

Seine-Port: Foire à la Brocante, first Sunday of every month.

VISITING THE ILE-DE-FRANCE

WHERE TO STAY

All of the Ile-de-France is easily accessible from Paris within two hours' driving time, so the region lends itself well to day trips. It is also ideal, nevertheless, as a weekend destination. Stopping over for one or two nights gives the visitor ample time to explore a portion of the Ile-de-France at leisure.

Chateau d'Esclimont, 28700 Saint-Symphorien-le-Château (near Ablis). Tel. 37 31 15 15 or 37 31 58 06. A refined and elegant 17th-century château-hotel set on vast parklike grounds. Classically furnished rooms are spacious and airy. Formal restaurant.

Hostellerie Blanche-de-Castille, place des Halles, 91410 Dourdan. Tel. 64 59 68 92. A small hotel in the heart of the old city with comfortable rooms, a cheerful garden, and a good restaurant.

Hostellerie de Lys, rond point de la Reine, 60260 Lamorlaye. Tel. 44 21 26 19. Just three miles from Chantilly, a pretty country inn with 35 rooms bathed in a rural calm.

La Forestière, 1 avenue du Président Kennedy, 78100 Saint-Germain-en-Laye. Tel. 34 51 93 80 or 39 73 36 60. An attractive inn set at the edge of the Forêt Saint Germain, with 24 rooms and six apartments, most opening onto a lush garden. Rooms traditionally furnished with colorful fabrics on walls. Home of the one-Michelin-star restaurant Cazaudhore.

L'Aigle Noir, 27 place Napoleon Bonaparte, 77300 Fontainebleau. Tel. 64 22 32 65. A pleasant in-town hotel facing Fontainebleau's majestic château (some rooms overlook the château, others a garden), luxuriously furnished in styles that span the eras of Louis XVI to the Restoration.

Le Pavillon Henri IV, 21 rue Thiers, 78100 Saint-Germain-en-Laye. Tel. 34 51 62 62. An elegant *hôtel de luxe* with 42 enormous rooms set at the edge of a vast, verdant park.

Le Vieux Logis, 105 rue de Paris, 60700 Fleurines, Pont-Sainte-Maxence (four miles from Senlis). Tel. 44 54 10 13. A small inn with only two large rooms overlooking a garden, niched in an idyllic setting at the edge of a forest. Notable for its rustic restaurant and warm welcome.

WHERE TO EAT

CHANTILLY
Le Relais Condé
42 avenue de Maréchal Joffre.
Tel. 44 57 05 75.
Closed Monday.

DOURDAN
Le Pot D'Argent
2 rue Saint Germain.
Tel. 64 59 40 20.
Closed Monday dinner and Tuesday.

JOIGNY
A La Côte St. Jacques
14 Faubourg Paris.
Tel. 86 62 09 70.
Open daily.

JOUY-EN-JOSAS
Fondation Cartier, Restaurant du Château
3 rue de la Manufacture.
Tel. 39 56 46 46.
Lunch only; closed Saturday and Sunday except during summer months.

MAISONS-LAFFITTE
Le Tastevin
9 avenue Eglé.
Tel. 39 62 11 67.
Closed Monday dinner and Tuesday.

La Vieille Fontaine
8 avenue Gretry.
Tel. 39 62 01 78.
Closed Monday.

MARLY-LE-ROI
Auberge du Vieux Marly
3 place du Général de Gaulle.
Tel. 39 58 47 70.
Closed Tuesday dinner and Wednesday.

Les Gourmandins
2 place de la Halle.
Tel. 44 60 94 01.
Closed Monday dinner and Tuesday.

MONTFORT-L'AMAURY
Les Préjugés
18 place Robert Brault.
Tel. 34 86 92 62.
Closed Tuesday.

POISSY
L'Esturgeon
6 cours du 14 Juillet.
Tel. 39 65 00 04.
Closed Thursday.

PONTCHARTRAIN
L'Aubergade
Route N12.
Tel. 34 89 02 63.
Closed Wednesday.

PROVINS
Quat' Saisons
44 rue du Val.
Tel. 64 08 99 44.

VERSAILLES
Brasserie du Théâtre
15 rue des Réservoirs.
Tel. 39 50 03 21.
Open daily.

Le Potager du Roy
1 rue du Maréchal Joffre.
Tel. 39 50 35 34.
Closed Sunday and Monday.

Rotisserie de la Boule d'Or
25 rue du Maréchal Foch.
Tel. 39 50 22 97.
Open daily.

FESTIVALS, FAIRS, AND RE-LIGIOUS EVENTS

Dates for these annual events often change from year to year. For precise dates, contact the Bureau de Tourisme in each town, or the French National Tourist Office, 630 Fifth Avenue, New York, NY 10019.

JANUARY

Provins: Fête de Saint Paul (Saint Paul Wine Festival), on the last weekend in January, in even years.

le parc et le musée sont fermés aujourd'hui

FEBRUARY

Chambly: Fête Folklorique du Bois-Hourdy (Folk Festival), the Sunday following Mardi Gras.

MARCH

Coulommiers: Foire Internationale aux Fromages et aux Vins de France (International Wine and Cheese Fair), late March.

MAY

Provins: Festival de Musique (Music Festival), end of May to end of June.

Rambouillet: Fête du Muguet (Lily of the Valley Festival), third Sunday in May.

JUNE

Bièvres: Foire à la Photo et Marché d'Occasion de la Photographie (Photo Fair and Photography Market), a weekend near June 15.

Bièvres: Fête de la Fraise (Strawberry Festival), one weekend in mid-June.

Le Vésinet: Fête de la Marguerite (Daisy Festival), second Sunday of June.

Brie Comte-Robert: Fête des Roses (Rose Festival), first Sunday of June, if it is not Pentecost.

Chantilly: Prix du Jockey Club (Jockey Club Horse Race), first or second Sunday in June.
Prix de Diane (Prix de Diane Cup Horse Race), second or third Sunday in June.

Conflans-Sainte-Honorine: Pardon Nationale de la Battellerie (Pardon and Mass on the Water), last or next-to-last Sunday in June.

Marcoussis: Fête de la Fraise (Strawberry Festival), third Sunday in June.

Marly: Le Grand Jet de Marly (the Marly Fountain Concerts), in Marly Park, fourth Sunday of May, June, July, August, and September, at 4:30 P.M.

JULY

Moret-sur-Loing: Spectacle de l'Eté (Summer Sound and Light Spectacular), Saturday evenings along the banks of the Loing, July 1–September 15.

Saint-Germain-en-Laye: Fête des Loges (Summer Festival), July 1–August 15.

AUGUST

Provins: Fête de la Moisson (Harvest Festival), last weekend in August.

SEPTEMBER

Arpajon: Foire aux Haricots (Green Bean Festival), from the Friday preceding to the Monday following the third Sunday in September.

Croissy-sur-Seine: Fête de la Carotte (Carrot Festival), between the first and second Sunday in September.

Montlhéry: Foire à la Tomate (Tomato Festival), second weekend of September.

OCTOBER

Achères: Fête du Céleri (Celery Festival), second half of October.

Rambouillet: Fête Equestre (Equestrian Festival), early October.

Saint-Augustin: Foire de la Pomme et du Cidre (Apple and Cider Festival), end of october.

Suresnes: Fête des Vendanges (Grape Harvest Festival), early October.

DECEMBER

Mantes-la-Jolie: Foire aux Oignons (Onion Fair), first Wednesday of December.

WEEKLY MARKETS

Lively and colorful open markets where farmers truck in the freshest fruit, vegetable, dairy, and meat products to be sold at small stands, usually manned by the growers themselves.

Auvers-sur-Oise: Saturday and Thursday.

Beauvais: Saturday and Wednesday.

Bièvres: Saturday and Wednesday.

Bougival: Saturday and Wednesday.

Brie-Comte-Robert: Thursday, Friday, and Sunday.

Chantilly: Wednesday and Saturday.

Chatou: Thursday through Sunday.

Coulommiers: Saturday and Sunday.

Dourdan: Wednesday and Saturday.

Dreux: daily, except Thursday and Saturday.

Enghien-les-Bains: Tuesday, Thursday, and Saturday.

Fontainebleau: Thursday, Friday, and Sunday.

Jouy-en-Josas: Tuesday and Friday.

Maisons-Laffitte: Wednesday and Saturday.

Marly-le-Roi: Tuesday, Friday, and Sunday.

Meaux: Saturday.

Milly-la-Forêt: Thursday.

Montfort l'Amaury: Thursday.

Poissy: Tuesday, Thursday through Sunday.

Provins: Saturday.

Rambouillet: Wednesday through Sunday.

Rueil-Malmaison: Tuesday, Friday, and Saturday.

Saint-Germain-en-Laye: Friday and Sunday.

Senlis: Tuesday and Friday.

Versailles: Tuesday, Thursday through Sunday.

WHAT TO SEE AND DO

The province of the Ile-de-France is not endowed with as many spectacular natural sights as some other provinces—Brittany and Normandy, for example—but the area is nevertheless rich in artistic, architectural, cultural, and historic places of interest. Among the sights and landmarks we suggest you take in while visiting the Ile-de-France are:

Anet: the imposing 16th-century castle, the Château d'Anet, built for Diane de Poitiers and the setting for her romance with her much younger lover, Henri II.

Chantilly: the château, the Musée Vivant du Cheval, and Le Hameau in the château park.

Giverny: the small village dominated by Claude Monet's enchanting homestead and recently restored gardens—more spectacular, if possible, than the painter's images themselves.

Jouy-en-Josas: home of the Oberkampf Museum in the Château de Montebello, with centuries of handsome hand-printed fabrics on display and in private archives.

Malmaison: Napoleon's Directoire residence decorated by Josephine, and nearby the Musée du Bois-Preau.

Rambouillet: the Bergerie and La Laiterie—the Sheep Farm and Marie Antoinette's Dairy—on the grounds of the vast château.

Royaumont: a serene 11th-century monastery, founded by Saint Louis (Louis IX), and today the setting for many concerts, lectures, antiques shows, and other cultural events.

Versailles: in addition to the dazzling palace, don't miss Marie Antoinette's Le Hameau, the Potager du Roy—the king's kitchen garden—and the small lively open market in town.

Traditional Ile-de-France towns with distinct character and architectural integrity: Auvers-sur-Oise, Beaumont-sur-Oise, Dourdan, Dreaux, Montargis, Montfort-l'Amaury, Moret-sur-Loing, Poissy, Provins, Senlis.

Several small museums that give an intriguing peek into the life and history of old Ile-de-France, with arts, crafts, costumes, interior design, and lifestyle: Musée de la Céramique, Sèvres; Musée du Château, Dourdan; Musée Départementale du Prieuré, Saint-Germain-en-Laye; Musée de l'Ile-de-France, Sceaux; Musée Marmottan, Boulogne; Musée Municipale, Neuilly; Musée du Provinois, Provins.

Many public gardens and parks dot the Ile-de-France, and make a fine destination for a weekend picnic:
Jardins de Vaux-le-Vicomte, 77950 Maincy
Jardins de Rambouillet, 78120 Rambouillet
Parcs et Jardins de Versailles, Parc Balbi, 78000 Versailles
Jardins de Saint-Germain-en-Laye, 78100 Saint-Germain-en-Laye
Jardins de Bagatelle, Bois de Boulogne, Paris
Parc de Sceaux, 92330 Sceaux
Jardins de Thoiry, 78770 Thoiry-en-Yvelines
Parc de Raray, 60810 Barbery
Parc de Malmaison, 92500 Rueil-Malmaison
Parc Vilmorin, 91370 Vilmorin

INDEX